JUST WHAT I NEEDED

JUST WHAT I NEEDED

DAILY DEVOTIONAL

ADREAN "PASTOR A" YOUNG

J. Merrill
PUBLISHING

J Merrill Publishing, Inc., Columbus 43207
www.JMerrill.pub

Published 2021

Library of Congress Control Number: 2021901185
ISBN-13: 978-1-950719-86-0 (Paperback)
ISBN-13: 978-1-950719-85-3 (eBook)

Title: Just What I Needed
Author: Adrean Young
Cover: Toya Jackson

To God first goes the glory for all of the things he has done! Without Him, there is no inspiration.

His blessing of my wife, Crystal, has grounded me and given me the extra will to accomplish this dream.

To my family, Kayla, Kiersten, Mom and dad, Brandon, Toya, Quaneta, Vincent, and Chenita: You have given me the love and joy to keep me pressing on.

To Jason, my other brother, you kept me in my word and showed me what a man of God looks like, even if it meant eating my green beans, lol.

Lastly, Jackie Smith Jr., thank you for listening to the Holy Spirit and trusting me to give you my dream.

I love you all! Thank you!

Last but definitely not least, Heart of God Kingdom Ministry Church, I love you all! Thank you for your returned love and support. I could not do this without what you have helped form in me! Monica Idom, you already know. Everyone needs a Journey in their life, and I am blessed to have one!

INTRODUCTION

For the last two years, I've been blessed to send inspirational messages to many individuals every morning.

In that, I have to send them individually; the spirit of God changes a few of the messages so that not everyone gets the same message every day. Because of that, I wanted this book to be written so that the spirit of God can give you exactly what you need for the day you read the inspiration.

Psalm 3:5-6 says, "we will trust God and let Him direct the beginning of our day by meditating on Him and listen for a number." When you have turned to the inspiration associated with your number, read it, and highlight or mark it to show it has already been read.

Does this mean God will not direct you back to the same one? No! He has given me the same message for over a month before.

What it will do is use the gifts that have been blessing me over the last few years to give you just what you need! As you move through the year, God will continue to enlighten your day with a perfect message for your moment!

Every message has been the result of praying and seeking God, every morning and He in return gave manna for the day!!

I pray it blesses you!

Pastor A!

Day 1

I t's your time! Get up and go get it! You have been set up to be successful this morning! New day, new mercy, and Jesus is waiting to lead you into your victory! Don't fear and don't delay! Move and go get it!

I love you!

https://youtu.be/ADGnIi9KrLQ[1]

---

1. Mary Mary TV, Mary Mary - Go Get It (Official Video)

Day 2

When a ship is sinking, it will suck you down with it if you're holding on or too close. So, even if you intended to get away from it and you stayed too close or started too late in your attempt to move, you will go down with it regardless.

Preacher, what are you saying?

It's time to let go of some things before it's too late! Those ships in your life are sinking. Don't go down with the ship!

It used to be seen as honorable for a captain to go down with a ship, but I am telling you right now that there is no honor in not trying to be saved!

Did you get the wisdom of that?

God has given you everything you need to survive and has told you many times if you let go, He will take over!

Take Him at His promises and let go!

I love you!

https://youtu.be/xGWu8OYzjjY[1]

---

1. INCHRIST WORSHIP, PJ Morton x The Walls Let Go & Let God

Day 3

Effort! That is a word that many forget is necessary for us to activate our faith. Faith without works is dead, so there must be some work. Let's concentrate on being diligent in making an effort towards the things that make us better saints! More effort in love, in kindness, in the will of God, on purpose! We can make it if we try! I love you!

https://youtu.be/sRsMhbFuoko[1]

---

1. Malacomg, Bishop Jeff Banks & The Revival Temple Mass Choir - You Can Make It If You Try

Day 4

Yesterday, "God said He would be a bridge over troubled water, but He never promised you wouldn't get wet...." This is why we have to stop letting our physical eyes and ears direct our faith! What did God say?! It doesn't matter what the media, social media, so-called friends, and even some family try to show or tell you! Let the Holy Ghost direct your faith! So do this, shout now! You already won! It is over! Give your faith a boost and pre-praise right now! I love you!

https://youtu.be/SMaFb8tAslA[1]

1. Mama's Gospel, don't wait till the battle's over shout now walter hawkins love alive choir 3

Day 5

You must know you can make it because the blood covers you. The enemy wants to use your past and memories to beat you and prevent you from inheriting your promises. Still, God wants you to remember this morning that He has saved you and put you in place to be blessed! You are saved from the penalty of your transgressions because His mercy has been poured over you! New morning, New grace, no going back! Always remember He has you in His arms! I love you!

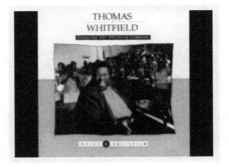

https://youtu.be/C64oYCnYvqU [1]

1. Gospel Tunes, 'We Remember (Medley)' Thomas Whitfield featuring The Whitfield Company

Day 6

It's amazing to be used by God. When you allow yourself to be the vessel and become His instrument, you also get blessed in return. How? Love in the place of vengeance, show mercy when none is deserved, give aide to one who refused to help you, pray for those that curse you, or give a kind word to someone who has tried to tear you down. Yes, this one is difficult, but you're not looking for them to give you anything in return. God's response is all you're worried about. No one can bless you like He can. I love you!

https://youtu.be/ftPOkDLNAEI[1]

1. Gospel Nostalgia, James Cleveland & the Charles Fold Singers (1979) "Lord Let Me An Instrument" Original Full Version

Day 7

Your eyes have opened, and now you get ready to face another day. That alone is a testimony of how good Jesus has been to you! Let your praise today begin with that. We used to say this, "I thank Him for waking me up in my right mind," and now we have forgotten how special that is. Look around you and see how much craziness in the world is happening, but you still can make sound decisions. That's another blessing. He has been so good already today! Give Him the praise! I love you!

https://youtu.be/_pXXqE-zyEw[1]

1. Malacomg, Willie Neal Johnson & the New Keynotes - Jesus You've Been Good To Me

Day 8

D on't stop fighting! God in you will win! You will win! Don't stop moving, pressing, and winning! We are His heirs, and we will get what is ours! It's time to win! Even in the midst of trouble and confusion, our God Has prepared us for this! Win! Win! Win! I love you!

https://youtu.be/o-R5hO3Uph4[1]

---

1. GROLTV, Pastor Monica and Family "You Fight On" again

Day 9

God deserves the glory! We can face today because He has graced us with one more day to win! Say this, "I will go into this day knowing I have already conquered whatever the enemy tries to use against me!" Then get excited and bless the name of the Lord who has delivered you today! He is good and greatly to be praised! I love you!

https://youtu.be/3iSPiKEmM50[1]

---

1. Fred Hammond, Glory To Glory To Glory

Day 10

The Spirit of God moved and told us last night that our victory is in our praise! So please don't wait to see it. Praise now in expectation! Give God equal praise! You're asking Him for a lot so let your praise match it! Go to it! Give Him His due "Hallel"! It will push your healing, peace, deliverance, desires, and restoration to you quicker as God loves our faith-based praise! Get yours this morning! I love you!

https://youtu.be/NKTpytkudvc[1]

---

1. Greater Is He That Is In Me, It's In The Praise - Calvin Bernard Rhone

Day 11

God will deliver you! From your cares, stresses, troubles, and pain. He will not leave you! When you are going through tests and trials, He will help you overcome! I promise you that He is waiting for you to lay everything on the altar of your heart so He can show you how much He loves you! Give it to Him today! You will not regret it! Peace, joy, healing, and victory are yours to have! I love you!

https://youtu.be/jvA-DU1okEcv[1]

---

1. Willie Ellebie Gospel Channel, He Delivered Me - The Rance Allen Group

Day 12

As we wait for a name to be declared for our country's leader, I am fully behind one name, Jesus! The name that has power and demons flee from! There is something about that name. When I was young and would be having a bad dream, I knew if I could just say "Jesus" in the dream, I could either turn it around or wake up. The enemy in the dreams would always fight to keep me from saying it. Even my subconscious knew where my power lays! I dare you to call Him for yourself!

I love you!

https://youtu.be/xlSZh-wsW6w[1]

1. Kirk Franklin, Something About The Name Jesus Pt. 2

Day 13

If you say you are a follower of Christ or a Christian, be the salt of the Earth as Jesus directed you to be. It's time to love one another above opinion and avoid the divisiveness that the enemy has tried so hard to instill. God is still God! That will not change with an election or any change man decides. We must continue to be the example of His wondrous love. I love you!

https://youtu.be/KdJZ1B_VIYc[1]

---

1. M Brown, John P. Kee-Salt of the Earth

Day 14

You are one of God's biggest miracles! You again have been granted new life this morning, and you didn't even have to feel the enemies attempt to kill you before you could wake up! Every day God puts you into places to receive His grace and favor, and even though you can't see it all of the time, His protection makes sure you can make it! It's time to give Him His due praise! We thank Him today! I love you!

https://youtu.be/pW7WoqIRC-Q[1]

---

1. Gospel Nostalgia, The Rance Allen Group (1991) "Miracle Worker"

Day 15

Don't stop now! You're going to make it! It doesn't matter what the world has told you! Your faith is stronger than your eyes! Let's hold each other up, praying, and running on! It's going to be alright as long as we keep moving! Jesus said it would be alright as long as we press toward his calling! Let's go! New morning, New mercies, New vision, New victory! I love you!

https://youtu.be/haAFrq6cpaQ[1]

---

1. Gospel Tunes, "I'll Make It" Hezekiah Walker & The Love Fellowship Crusade

Day 16

Sometimes you have to remind the devil that this isn't new to you! Sometimes you have to tell your situation, your surroundings, your haters, and some of those so-called friends you have been here before! You have had to face the obstacles and trials, and although they look like they have gotten ahead, you will praise your way out of it and watch the glory of the Lord prevail! I don't have to see it because I know what I heard God say! I'm not worried about it! In Him, I live, I breathe, and I am what I have been created to be! So right now, wherever you are, give God an "I know I win by knockout" praise! I don't know who the enemy thought he was in a fight with! He must have forgotten! I love you!

https://youtu.be/HfGSaTR9zEQ[1]

---

1. GOP Church, "It's Getting Ready to Happen" Praise Break - Elder Tyquan Sparks

Day 17

If you don't usually pay attention to these messages, I implore you to read this one! Why would you ask God for change in your life and then get mad at him and life for changing your friends and current situation? You must realize that God's plan for you and the change it requires involve only God's trusted to help cultivate your purpose.

When I was young, my cousin had a small Honda Civic that sat four people comfortably. The problem was, we were at least ten deep, and all wanted to go with him everywhere. We all wanted to go so bad that, no matter how illegal, we would all pile into that car because we wanted to go that bad. We fit 13 people one time. What's my point? If someone really wanted to ride with you on your journey for God, they will pile into your life and make themselves fit because it was important! There is a reason why God's way seems like a two-seater that your driving! Everybody can't go with you, and the ones that want to will fit! Respect the change, and go get your promise! I love you!

https://youtu.be/hPfYcy8zOUE[1]

---

1. Walter Hawkins - Topic, Changed

Day 18

Yesterday is over. Last week is over! Last month is over! Last year is over! Your past is not today! You have brand new mercy and undeserving grace to make sure your right now is a brand new beginning! So get up, wipe yourself off, and go recover what you "THOUGHT" you lost! Yes, your thought is just a trick of the enemy because no one can take what God has gifted to you! We sometimes listen to the voices and critics and lay things down but no more! Get your mind right! Pray, thank God for the chance to be back in His will and pick up what's yours and let's change the world! We are worried about an election, but God is concerned about your selection. Choose ye this day whom you will serve! If you let Him lead, the rest will take care of itself! Now let's recover it all, TODAY! I love you!

https://youtu.be/IgIp_ZICpqE[1]

---

1. Gene Moore TV, Gene Moore - Recover (Lyric Video)

Day 19

As for me and my house, we will serve the Lord! In a time and place when it is popular to allow children to explore their own way and spouses are independent although together, I decided a long time ago to put my house on a path to chase Jesus! He is our heart's desire, and we run to Him! I encourage you this morning to Seek Him More! If you do, you will find Him waiting to do more for you! Keep searching Him out in His Word and know the true Him for yourself! A true relationship with Him and your household brings a hedge around your home that keeps you in His arms! It is a beautiful place to reside! I love you!

https://youtu.be/jrDqi7HQzUc[1]

1. GospelMusicTV, Chasing After You (The Morning Song)- Tye Tribbett & G.A.

Day 20

G et up! It doesn't matter what's coming; you've got the victory! Nothing coming can conquer you as long as God is with you! The weapons are indeed formed and even used, but they can't defeat you! No fear, no doubt, no backing down! Let's break through today! It's time for our situations to work for the good of you! It's promised! So it is written, so it is done! I love you!

https://youtu.be/hnVB6t1Qek4[1]

---

1. Kirk Franklin, Kirk Franklin - 123 Victory (Audio)

Day 21

I love to watch MMA. One of the most dominant fighters ever retired undefeated this past weekend at 29-0. The stat that I want you to hear is this, as awesome as he was, two times he lost a round. Only twice! As amazing as that sounds, that means two times he had to endure the thought process of, "am I going to lose now? Has my career started to turn for failure?" He had the resolve to put those thoughts out and go back in and win to remain undefeated! The message, you have a saviour that has never been defeated. So why listen to the voices of the enemy because you may have lost a round? Jesus' record is greater than 29 and 0! You can not and will not lose! Be the champion he has created you to be! I love you!

https://youtu.be/UGa5rpcMG2M[1]

---

1. Rich Tolbert Jr., Rich Tolbert Jr. - Never Be Defeated (Official Audio)

Day 22

Loving others is what is very important and necessary in our world today! When we understand that others' imperfections are just like our own, and we all need God to fix us, it makes it easy to love one another. If you're too perfect for this, I am not talking to you. But if you are like me and have been forgiven for a few things, some that I'm glad God has allowed to stay between us, then let's love each other! Make a point to tell someone you love them today! Oh, I love you, by the way!

https://youtu.be/Ve8rVcCfxb4[1]

---

1. DeMarcus Merritt, The Walls Group- Perfect People (Lyric Video)

Day 23

My message this morning is in the words of this song. Please enjoy. Let it speak to you. I love you!

https://youtu.be/t6CdvJseUiA[1]

---

1. Lakeyshuh Carolina, Better By Jessica Reedy lyric video

Day 24

The song I'm sending is exactly where my inspiration is this morning. I love you

https://youtu.be/BxxKFECN7EU[1]

---

1. Gaither Music TV, Smokie Norful - I Need You Now (Live)

Day 25

I can make it because of him! There is no way I would try without him! Win with him today! Love you!

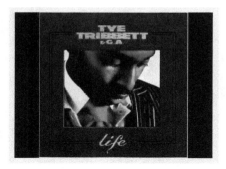

https://youtu.be/QO3A1pGhdXY[1]

---

1. JAFProductions, Tye Tribbett - No Way

Day 26

Say this, this morning, "Nothing will stop me today!" Now stand on it and believe it! God created you to be unstoppable! Life and death reside in the power of your tongue. Greater is He that is in you than he that is in the world. In Him, you live, move, and have your being! That adds up to you can accomplish anything! Time to push doubt out and to press on! Don't stop now! You keep running the race! You've got this! I love you!

https://youtu.be/l5sbTKf7_NE[1]

---

1. Lowell Pie - Topic, Keep Pressing

Day 27

In such a time like this, we need to hear the Spirit lead. The Holy Ghost's indwelling is especially important now in a world that has an agenda against the very will of God. When our lives are challenged to accept hate over love and choose easy over right, we need God's Spirit to dwell in our every decision. Lord, you guide and lead us this day and forevermore, in Jesus' name! I love you!

https://youtu.be/Nj4_JHHuOls[1]

---

1. Enni Francis, Oceans | Hillsong | Cover | by Enni Francis ft Kanaan Francis|

Day 28

It's time to face the day with your new mercy in hand and your faith in front, ready for the challenges that you may face, knowing you've got a close friend who has made it clear you win! It's not about how perfect you can be compared to anyone else. It's about being redeemed from the sins of this world and having the perfecter living on the inside! This helps you love better, stand bolder, pray more, and live Holy! Your redemption was bought and paid for in blood! Now walk with the confidence that you know your redeemer is winning this day for you! It doesn't matter how yesterday ended! Jesus is on the case! I love you!

https://youtu.be/UWlgjFYSaQA[1]

1. Isaac Carree, Simply Redeemed

Day 29

It's personal between God and me! He knows my secrets, my thoughts, my desires, and my failures. I tell Him everything! Not because he doesn't already know them but because that's what close friends do! Our line of communication is wide open, but I don't do all of the talking. I spend a lot of time just listening. Is that your relationship with Him? If not, you aren't experiencing the best part of Jesus! The part where He tells you how much He loves you and you feel His arms wrapped around you, protecting you, loving you. If you want to feel this, get into the Word of God! Read it like the love letter to you that it is! I promise you that He will speak! I love you!

https://youtu.be/6F8IuJcWbA8[1]

---

1. Tonex - Topic, Personal Jesus

Day 30

L uke 1:37 says For, with God, nothing is impossible. That means the voices you hear saying you can't, you won't, and it's over are lies! You don't have to believe the enemy's narrative! You walk with the greatest force ever known, and He has told you that your change is in the power of your tongue! Speak that thing, and let's shout together! I love you!

https://youtu.be/rDo2TFfmuvU[1]

Day 31

It's time to be free! Your bonds have been loosened by a saviour who has made your current situation another testimony! Your faith has brought you here. Now watch Jesus do the rest! Walk into your freedom today! I love you!

https://youtu.be/Y_ryOncTbBo[1]

Day 32

I magine what we could accomplish, get through, or begin if we would abolish fear. The enemy has intended our fear so well that we have made it a regular part of our daily process. Fear keeps you from even hearing the directions from God. It's time to kick fear out! That spirit is not welcome anymore! By the power of the blood of Jesus, we step out of any fear now! Now walk boldly in faith today! I love you!

https://youtu.be/euMgUotevog[1]

---

1. Brian Courtney Wilson, Brian Courtney Wilson - Fear Is Not Welcome (Lyric Video)

Day 33

S tand on your faith! We used to say, "If you pray, don't worry, and if you worry, why pray?" If you already asked the one true God for a solution, healing, a way out, or whatever the request was, trust that He will deliver! Your faith is important! Without it, there is no way to please God! You don't need much, but you must have it and keep it! Don't worry! We already prayed! I love you!

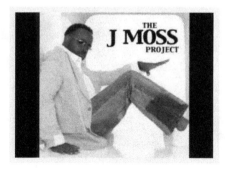

https://youtu.be/LMwcoMYVVA4[1]

---

1.   Maurie McDonald, J Moss - Don't Pray & Worry

Day 34

There is nobody like the Lord! I dare you to try Him as I have! You will find out you have a friend who will always have your back, front, side, and every angle the enemy thinks he can slide in! You have the opportunity to make Jesus your best friend today! Don't miss out! I love you!

https://youtu.be/cB4z2Zk8ukw[1]

---

1. PrazHymn83, Fred Hammond - Nobody Like You, Lord

Day 35

I t's your time! Whatever it is God has positioned you for, do it! Make the moves! Your moves will make a change in your life and the lives around you! Stop hearing the noise that's trying to distract you and push through to what you know has been designed for you! You will be happier and whole! Jesus is with you in his will, so press into it and let's move!

https://youtu.be/kuMitvUWfko[1]

---

1. The Winans - Topic, It's Time

Day 36

We can do everything because of God's grace and mercy! Granted, what we never could earn and avoid punishment we did deserve because of His love! His mercy starts new with you new every morning so take advantage of it! He set up your success, and now it's time for you to walk in it! Win today! I love you!

https://youtu.be/Mxz-c8MLAoU[1]

1. Malacomg, The Mississippi Mass Choir - Your Grace And Mercy

Day 37

K eep holding on to God! He is unchanging and will never leave you! People will flake out and change their support and opinions, but God is the constant that will provide stability to your life if you let Him! People will not appreciate you and will let you down, but God's grace will favor you even when the report is against you! You can make it and be more than blessed even in times like these! Just don't let go of His hands! I promise He will not change! I love you!

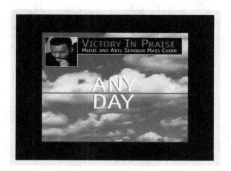

https://youtu.be/l6LDLQRzbog[1]

---

1. CTPannell Traditional Gospel Music, Hold On (God's Unchanging Hand) - John P. Kee, VIP Music & Arts Seminar Mass Choir

Day 38

As you're up this morning, give God a great thank you! It could have been a different story and circumstance for you, but you are in a home, car, on your phone, food to eat, doing better than someone else! He deserves the praise! Always remember what it should have been before God's grace changed your verdict! Rejoice in your trials because you can have them! He is still there with you! He loves you, and I do too!

https://youtu.be/VQDKImkt2Qs[1]

---

1. Bengo940, 8.Kirk Franklin ft J.Moss & Tye Tribbett - Could've been me

Day 39

If you ever thought or wondered how I keep pressing through, know it's not always easy, but Jesus is the reason! He is the first person I call when trouble arises, and He is the first I thank when great things happen! I depend on Him, and He always sees me through. I dare you to try Him truly! If you need His number, I can forward it to you! He will not let you down! I love you!

https://youtu.be/dowKahcGcLY[1]

---

1. Milton Brunson - Topic, Guess You're Wondering

Day 40

Don't let go! Your change is right there! God has not let you down! His timing is impeccable! Right when the enemy thought you were going down! He didn't see the uppercut coming! I told you before; God heard you the first time! He just needed you to believe it! Hold on and walk in your victory! I love you!

https://youtu.be/V24-3bSoa2I[1]

---

1. AndyMatch, Sounds Of Blackness - Hold On (Change Is Comin') (Roger Troutman's Remix)

Day 41

Do you realize that Jesus is looking out for you? Even now? You think things are bad, but He is keeping it from being worse! "Why can't he take it all, so you don't have to go through any of it," you ask? He is saying, "Why can't they see, with the faith they tell everyone they have, that I have set up their next testimony and I have reinforced their strength and resolve to make it while I fight through it for them!" He has you on His mind! He hasn't left you! Your still here! That should be enough for you to see His design in you! I love you!

https://youtu.be/S6WO3pnEGBo[1]

---

1. Kirk Franklin, Lookin' Out For Me

Day 42

I am overwhelmed with gratitude this morning for a saviour who paid a cost with my name on it. I was heading towards death and a punishment worthy of the life I had lived to that point, and He saved me from it all even though I did nothing to deserve it. All I did was ask and gave Him my heart and acknowledged who He is and what He did for me. My heart is full of love and joy because it is my pleasure to represent such love and sacrifice. How about you? Your cost of bad decisions and bad living have been rectified by a Jesus who volunteered to die to pay the debt. Now how do you show gratitude? I'm going to worship some more this morning because of it! Join me! I love you!

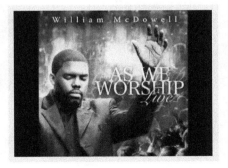

https://youtu.be/yZ2u15TEk_o[1]

---

1. Kassiedoo, William McDowell - Here I Am To Worship

Day 43

God's got you! It looks hard or undoable, but I am telling you now that He is there with you! No other power can defeat Him, and He is on your side! Walk in it! I love you!

https://youtu.be/VQ-_uGePfzQ[1]

---

1. Bryce Brown, Donald Lawrence - I am God

Day 44

Get up! Time to win again! You had a friend fighting for you while you slept! Did you forget you weren't in this by yourself? Dig in and gird up! Yes, it's a fight, but you've been equipped and built for this! God's got you! Let's go! You won already! Greater is He that is in you; Go, Win! I love you!

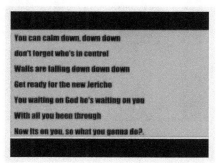

https://youtu.be/4alkB5yyw9o[1]

---

1.   Lyrics World, Kirk Franklin- 123 Victory Lyrics!!!

Day 45

If God said it, count on it! No more listening to the noise from the peanut gallery! One voice, one vision, it's all God's, and we follow! We are a people! All over the world, all different with different jobs focused on one purpose, God's will! That means what God has told you to do is important to the purpose! Stop letting other folks hate and doubt interrupt your destiny! He wrote the vision and made it plain, so you run into it! I love you!

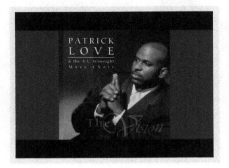

https://youtu.be/SWM9ef5LNXk[1]

---

1. Patrick Love & The A.L. Jinwright Mass Choir - Topic, The Vision

Day 46

I t was never about you! It has always been about who you affect! It's time to let your life and your daily journey be the change! We serve! Our ability to provide for and help others is the essential purpose of our Christian lives. We serve as Christ served! That's your mission today! Let's serve! I love you!

https://youtu.be/M_ak-4SQ_FE[1]

---

1. Jerome Hunt, Jermaine Dolly - Serve Official Video

Day 47

Thankful this morning. With everything going wrong in the world, I am awake and able to put a few coherent sentences together, which is a blessing in itself. Let us give God true praise for His goodness and favor. I promise you it will change the tone of your day! Thank Him now, then thank me later!?? I love you!

https://youtu.be/xXjyuNBWujM[1]

---

1. RachaelLampaVideos, Rachael Lampa - Blessed - acoustic performance (@rachaellampa)

Day 48

It only matters what God says you are! If He has labeled you, titled you, gifted you, called you, then walk in His words and be exactly that! Stop letting people and the devil discourage you by their foolish antics and ploys to make you fall! Haters gonna hate! It's time to rise above the noise and hear what God says! There is peace in hearing it! I love you!

https://youtu.be/sIaT8Jl2zpI[1]

---

1. Lauren Daigle, Lauren Daigle - You Say (Official Music Video)

Day 49

"I will praise Him until I break through!" That's what a believer speaks in a place of patience! When you can elevate your faith to a place where you praise and worship even though what you see has no good end, that's when God's eternal grace and mercy meet you in your moment. Your patience will be rewarded by God's deliverance and then some! I have seen it for myself! God responds! You may not understand it sometimes but know that his answer is always for the kingdom's betterment! So keep patiently praising! He has you covered!

https://youtu.be/po_44oy_TSs[1]

---

1. Fred Jerkins - Topic, Patiently Praising (feat. Lowell Pye)

Day 50

God gets the glory! Even in the midst of our world's despair, God still provides! He is awesome and is worthy of our praise! The more you thank him, the more he finds more to give you! You may have a lot, or you may be in need. Still, whatever you find yourself facing, the goodness of God, especially when appropriated, falls freshly! So praise Him! I love you!

https://youtu.be/B_9qAF7buro[1]

---

1. TheSoulSeekersMusic, The Soul Seekers ft. Marvin Winans "It's All God" Official Music Video

Day 51

Are you overloaded? Is the pressure getting to you? I promise you that you have a friend waiting to tag into your wrestling problems so He can relieve you of the pressure! Try Jesus for real! He wins! Go to Him this morning, pray Him into your situation, leave Him in it, and don't buy it back by still trying it your way. It will make a difference! Trust me! I love you!

https://youtu.be/Gjfs3rSIpIQ[1]

---

1. Sounds of Blackness - Topic, The Pressure Pt. 1

Day 52

Jesus knew you would be valuable before you were born, so why have you let the world around you tell you otherwise? Know your worth! You are so valuable that the enemy has to use your past, your mind, and every false truth he can to try and stop your progress. If you take a million-dollar diamond and sell it for $5, it will not change its value! You may have felt like you weren't purchased for much but know this, Jesus didn't overpay! He knew you were worth every drop of blood He shed! I love you! Live worthy!

https://youtu.be/iX59fjowutw[1]

---

1. Tyscot, Anthony Brown & group therAPy - Worth (Official Music Video)

Day 53

I am assured that I have found the one way to everything my heart has yearned for! Jesus is the way! He will never leave or ignore me. He has proven himself every day. If your testimony is anything like mine, you have reminded yourself that you shouldn't even be here, except by His goodness and mercy! If you feel lost, depressed, anxious, overwhelmed, hurt, or just blah, I encourage you to try Jesus! He is the way! He will lead you out, deliver your mind, heal your body, grant you peace! Stop depending on people and your own decisions! That's a quick way to temporary and false satisfaction! I promise that Jesus is what you need! I love you!

https://youtu.be/mxJzt3qZ-JM[1]

---

1. Jason Taylor, Here II Praise: He Is The Way

Day 54

Only the enemy uses your past against you! Many will pray to God, saying, "I am so sorry for all of those things I did before I got saved, but I keep feeling so bad about what I used to do, so Lord help me." And God's response is, "What are you talking about? I cast all of those things away from memory. So if I don't remember, you don't have to either! Live forward in me and not backward in pain!" When God cleans you, he completes the job! Walk in your new mercy this morning, and have a brand new morning and day! You're clean now, so walk squeaky clean in him today! I love you!

https://youtu.be/KgzxoGS9YNU[1]

1. Ctina323, Clean Inside by Bishop Hezekiah Walker and the Love Fellowship Crusade Choir

Day 55

You have already won! You have the victory! Make your joy known! Proclaim your desire and praise him now! We know that His joy will fill you even though the world around you sees with tainted vision. Count it all joy! Man's defeat still leads to God's victories! I will praise Jesus anyhow! The blessings are too many not to! I love you!

https://youtu.be/ToRiyYbs5Ro[1]

---

1. MrsMusic912, The Winans - Count It All Joy

Day 56

I realize that when the moments in my life have gotten big, it is never me alone that has accomplished anything. Jesus in me has been the success I have needed! From sports to music to speaking to just being a father, I have leaned on Him, and He always has come through! I am taking this moment to acknowledge that if Jesus wasn't there, I would fall! My hope, faith, success, and everything is built on, in, and through Him! Take a moment to let Him know this morning that you appreciate Him. Watch your desires become a reality just because you continue to lean on Jesus! I love you!

https://youtu.be/vCC18CnwDv4[1]

1. Kadeem Graves, If You Move, I'll Fall - The Bolton Brothers

Day 57

You are loved! You didn't have to earn it or deserve it. All you have to do is accept it and love in return. The love of Jesus has saved your life before you knew you needed saved but have you tried to experience the love fully? I challenge you to try! You will love me for it, I promise! By the way, I love you!

https://youtu.be/RBzxTYW5LGU[1]

---

1. Kadeem Graves, Unconditional - Fred Hammond & Radical For Christ

Day 58

Though you may not understand it now, God is working it out in your favor to go in line with your destiny! You don't have to see or hear it physically to be so! Just know that He always does what He promised, so don't try to use your own logic or reasoning. Lean on the Word in you, the faith in you, and the Holy Spirit in you! Say this, this morning, "I will lean on my Jesus because He has my life in His hands!" Now, that's the way to start the day! I love you!

https://youtu.be/_IglNCYgeEA[1]

---

1. Derrick Green, Leon Timbo I Lean Not On My Own Understanding Nothing I Hold on Too

Day 59

As you begin another day, realize Jesus is your victory and protection. He is your bridge over obstacles, trials, and attacks you never even see. Praise him for what you don't experience just as much as when you go through. Just have the faith and stay in His will and know when you have times of peace, he took on the battle for you! I love you!

https://youtu.be/_9-yfeA2JZs[1]

---

1. Revival, Aretha Franklin - Bridge Over Troubled Water

Day 60

This is not where your story ends! This isn't where you are supposed to doubt or give up! God is quickening your spirit this morning and telling you to get moving! It's closing time! We must finish strong! The race isn't over! We are on the backstretch, but there is a lot of running yet to do! Your destiny is now! Your time is now! God said it and I believe it! I love you!

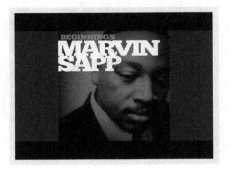

https://youtu.be/-sIAjm9XlN8[1]

---

1. Marvin Sapp, Not The Time, Not The Place (Ult Version)

Day 61

J ust a reminder this morning, God is still with you! You are not alone. Now let Him show you what it is to be taken care of by Him! That doesn't mean you won't face trouble. It means trouble won't win! I love you!

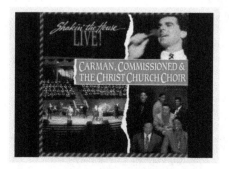

https://youtu.be/c8tSOi68Wv4[1]

---

1. Cheek Life, I Am Here - Commissioned 'Live'

Day 62

How do you want your morning, day, or week to go? Do you want peace, joy, or victory? In the middle of whatever you're facing, do you want the assurance that you're not alone? Of course, you do! So it's time for you to set your atmosphere around you to be the environment you need. Your worship does this! Your praise seals it! Your praying prepares your way, and the Word in you allows you to hold on to it! You win your day starting now! Holy Ghost, set it now! I love you!

https://youtu.be/hkSTd8ETUfo[1]

---

1. Chelsea Blair, Kurt Carr ~ Set the Atmosphere

Day 63

It's time for a recharge! The Lord is ready to refill, restore, and replenish what you have poured out and used up in your life. He is ready to breathe life into you and revive you! You just have to sit still long enough to charge. Feel His spirit Flow through you now as he breathes life into your worn-out spirit! If you're tired but haven't done anything, that's a message for a different day. But if you're on the battlefield and feel like you can't raise your arms many more times, feel Him breathe now! I love you!

https://youtu.be/OXiKı-84RHs[1]

---

1. Cheek Life, Breathe into Me Oh Lord - Fred Hammond

Day 64

Simply put, Jesus is my everything. I can't live, move, or do anything without him. I will worship him in the face of trouble, criticism, and attack because he will be victorious in it all! Will you stand for him? Let the redeemed of the Lord say so! Is He your all? Then say so! I love you!

https://youtu.be/OAXXEdVhH8w[1]

---

1. Gardenboy32, TONY LEE AND UNITY LIVE

Day 65

My prayer is that the world sees all of Jesus in all of me. When I talk, when I work, when I play, in everything. My reflection should show a glowing image of Christ in me. Challenge yourself to show him in everything for this day. Can you show Him in everything you do without saying it? Let him come out in your love, cleanliness, and work ethic! It is the true ministry! I love you!

https://youtu.be/dhfFsj5ALNo[1]

---

1. YourMowf, Anointed - It's not the I but the You in Me

Day 66

It's time to win the day! Yes, you win it right now by telling God thank you for the victory, telling him your plan for the day, listening for his adjustments, heading out to do exactly what you've heard, knowing he approves it! You were created to win! Now let's go! I love you!

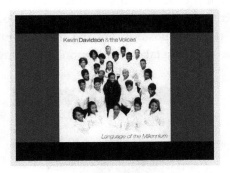

https://youtu.be/bLx9dG29pGI[1]

---

1. Kevin Davidson - Topic, Born To Win

Day 67

I t's time for a change, which means it's time for real prayer to go forth. I'm not talking about the cutesy, showy, very repetitive, and rehearsed prayers this time. I'm talking about the Holy Spirit led, on your knees or laying prostrate before Him, with moaning, crying, and some yelling. From the heart and soul and until you break through! I heard in my spirit someone say, "It doesn't take all of that." Well, like Elijah laying in the fetal position praying hard for rain, sometimes to undo what we have done, it takes a little more! Let's pray y'all! I love you!

https://youtu.be/9YZZzgJB33E[1]

---

1. Tauren Wells, Tauren Wells - When We Pray (Official Music Video)

Day 68

Your patience will be rewarded! Those that wait on Him shall renew their strength. I know your eyes are playing tricks on you, and things seem to be hard, but I promise if you hold on, God has something special brewing. All you have to do is wait on Him! He will show up on time! Be encouraged and wait! I love you!

https://youtu.be/Kq2mBzqQzvc[1]

---

1. The New Life Community Choir - Topic, Wait On Him

Day 69

I woke up to an unexpected thunderstorm. As the thunder thumped, the power turned off and back on. My mind was immediately taken to the process of, "where are the flashlights? I should have bought the generator. I hope this doesn't last, why on the Holiday..." Our lives have these scenarios constantly. During unexpected storms, our minds are checking to see if we prepared correctly. Well, be encouraged! You can tell the storm to render peace, and by your proclamation, you will have peace! Remember, though. It never said the clouds left, and the storm was gone. It said the winds and waves stopped, and there was calm. It can be a storm all around you, but Jesus can cause the storm for you to stop! Trust him in it! Your winds and waves must cease at your faith! I love you!

https://youtu.be/zzgTC5TS87Y[1]

---

1. Jeanetteaw, Dear Hurricane Ike- I TOLD THE STORM- LYRICS

Day 70

You say you trust God. Now it's time to live like it! Your stresses, cares, and problems have affected your health, decision making, and lifestyle. God is waiting for his people to live like they truly trust Him! No more depending on other things to do what He has promised. Check yourself! If you trust in anything other than Him for peace, love, joy, or anything, you have put something before Him. You must trust Him! I love you!

https://youtu.be/jMauOabTAfg[1]

---

1. CeddieCed, Men of Standard- Trust In God

Day 71

Its time! God ordained it! Why else would he have given you a new day? So let's go get it! Claim the day as a victory! It starts now! I love you!

https://youtu.be/ADGnIi9KrLQ[1]

---

1. Mary Mary Tv, Mary Mary - Go Get It (Official Video)

Day 72

A re you ready? Have you made room? Did you know it was your day? God has a blessing that was ordained for you specifically, ready today! Now you just have to walk in the faith of knowing it! Of course, the enemy will do everything to try to get you to give it up also willingly. Still, you must recognize what that is and smile through it, saying, "God's got a blessing for me, and I'm not giving it up!" Forgive, hold on, and keep the faith! Today is your breakthrough! I love you!

https://youtu.be/dHF5iqgvBwE[1]

---

1. HeartBeats Agape Church, God's Got A Blessing (lyrics)

Day 73

I am so glad I serve a living Saviour! He has proven Himself to me, and I will continue to praise Him and tell the world! When was the last time you felt Him? Has it been a while? If so, take a deep breath, look around, realize you just breathed Him in, and saw His handiwork. He is in the wind and sunshine. He is in everything around you! I dare you to take a moment this morning to appreciate Jesus and let Him move on you before you start your day! He is waiting for that chance! I love you!

https://youtu.be/PVRqNR9rayI[1]

---

1. Soulfuljakazz07, Mighty Clouds Of Joy- God Is Not Dead

Day 74

If you're changed, be changed! It's time for it to show! If you change your outfit, you should look completely different. That's common sense. Why do we believe God is ok with us saying we are changed, but we look, act, talk, and walk the same? We must be the change! Let the redeemed of God say so! Don't just say it, be it! I love you!

https://youtu.be/OnyjgYcGJ2E[1]

---

1. Walter Hawkins - Topic, Changed

Day 75

A re you still holding on? Have you made up in your mind to never give up? Can you make it? The Lord has desired that you hold on to His hand and never let go! He will carry you through your storm, and although the winds and rain will beat against you, He will keep you anchored! I'm still holding on, and He has kept me! Make up in your mind today to hold on! He will keep you too! I love you!

https://youtu.be/kN6Xtoo4cLQ[1]

---

1. JayEm86, "I'm Still Holding On" (1984)- Luther Barnes, Red Budd Choir

Day 76

I was looking through music for tomorrow's message, and the Spirit of God said someone needs it tonight. Your storm seems like it will never end, and you've been feeling like it's never going to stop. But, I want you to know if you just hold on through the night, your morning is coming! When I lived in Hawaii, there would be hard rains, but the Sun would be shining, and you would be able to see a rainbow too. This always would remind me that just because it was storming, I never had to worry because my promise and the Son would always be going through it with me! You're not alone! Jesus hasn't left you, and His promises are true! I love you!

https://youtu.be/BVmJV4JyyjU[1]

---

1. PeculiarPrayze, Vickie Winans - Rainbow

Day 77

Don't give up the fight! God hasn't quit on you! He is still fighting for you, so you can't stop! Your dreams, your purpose, and your anointing are worth fighting for! Make sure you fight for it! I love you!

https://youtu.be/tSD8IhFaIjo[1]

---

1. Global Gospel Group, Brian Courtney Wilson - Worth Fighting For

Day 78

God will not, does not, and has not failed! His timing is outside of our understanding. His sovereignty is beyond what we can imagine, but it will never fail! He will never fail you. You may not understand it now, but He will reveal in time! Just hold on and trust the Holy Ghost inside of you! He will never fail you! I love you!

https://youtu.be/4t7T5KTaHG8[1]

---

1. Gilbertmonk, Lowell Pye - Jesus Never Fails

Day 79

You're not alone! Jesus knows what you're going through! He wants to bear the weight of your burdens, but you have to let Him! I know it hurts, and I know you feel like you can't go on, but I want to tell you that He said, "I have heard you and now feel me hold you!" He purposely shed blood to eradicated your fear and loneliness! Your struggles died that day on Calvary! Don't pick them back up! Live free today! I love you!

https://youtu.be/hGFspf9IE8Y[1]

---

1. Cheek Life, Commissioned - Crucified With Christ

Day 80

Can you say that despite everything that Jesus is everything to you? The enemy is trying to take your eyes off of the goal! One thing about getting hit hard by an enemy, you either lay down and pray it's over, or you get angry and decide that you're going to make sure the hitter will never be able to chew food the same again; which one are you? (God gave you armor to use!) If you're the first type, I pray with you right now that your attack is over and I will fight for you. If you're the second, then let's get it! Time to fight! Fast, pray, read, love, worship, praise, testify, and repeat! The weapons of our warfare are not carnal! It's time to knock some walls down! I'm angry and motivated because the enemy has seen fit to make a consistent attack recently. It's our turn! Who's with me? I love you!

https://youtu.be/Tk8dMEn3PJY[1]

---

1. Denzeldavon2, Tye Tribbett & G.A. | Everything Part I,Part II / Bow Before The King

Day 81

In such a time as this, we need a word from the Lord! The climate has once again pitted everyone against each other, and there is no unity. Without unity, there is no strength, and the enemy is attacking while God's people are in disarray. A word of direction and love is what we need to hear. Open your heart and ears this morning so that it's His will we are following. We must remember love is the draw, not being the loudest! I love you!

https://youtu.be/fM5uu3zsUOI[1]

---

1. Thomas Whitfield - Topic, We Need A Word From The Lord

Day 82

If I called you, would you come running? If I was in trouble, would you come ready to help fight me out? Well, people of God, this season has left us standing in a time of trouble, and I am emitting out a war cry! It's time for the redeemed of the Lord to say so, and it's time to use the armor God has given you! Some may have to dust off a few items like the Breastplate of Righteousness or the Shield of Faith, but it's still yours and still functioning, so let's go! It's not the time for the timid or the scared! The War Cry has been sent out! How will you respond? I love you!

https://youtu.be/RjkFe-ronwc[1]

1. Micah Stampley, War Cry

Day 83

If your grounded in Jesus, no storm, wind, or wave can knock you off course. You may be tossed and shaken, but your anchor will hold you because God won't let you go. So make sure you are grounded in Him! Make sure you have the Word of God rooted on the inside. Make sure your prayer life reaches beyond saying grace and when you want something. Learn what fasting really is and practice it regularly. Then you will feel your anchor hold! I love you!

https://youtu.be/ENv7zIo_j9M[1]

---

1. Robbieatnsudotcom, My Soul Is Anchored by Douglas Miller

Day 84

We have made it through so much that it is important to give God the praise for favor! I can't help but get excited when I think about what He has done for me! I will forever give him praise through everything! What I am going through, no matter how hard, does not equal what He has already brought me through! It is just added to the list of testimonies! If you're not sure about that in your own life, begin to add up all he has kept from your doorstep too! He is worthy of the praise! I can't help it! I love you!

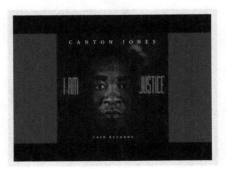

https://youtu.be/h7F-XLsZwis[1]

---

1. Canton Jones, I Can't Help It

Day 85

It's a new day. Breathe it in and realize the first blessing of this day, mercy. God has made sure He let you know this morning that you are not alone, and healing begins now. You look at this opportunity to feel His presence and know a better day than yesterday is your miracle from Him. "....I don't believe He brought me this far to leave me!" I love you!

https://youtu.be/OASpgmC-TsY[1]

---

1. Kirk Franklin, Brighter Day

Day 86

God has promised! That is a powerful statement. When you hear it, you realize that the next words have to come true. This day I am reminding you that He has made a promise to you and what comes next is what you have been waiting for! Your chains have to break! Your tears have to be paid for! Your joy has to return! Now walk in it! It's your time! I love you!

https://youtu.be/ucY6NwQTI3M[1]

---

1. Tasha Cobbs Leonard, Tasha Cobbs Leonard - Break Every Chain (Live At Passion City Church)

Day 87

I t's time for you to decide – waver or stand! The waves are high, and the wind is pressing against you. The Jesus you saw when you stepped out of the boat seems so far away. Your faith is shaken, but I'm encouraging you to know that he that dwells in the secret place of the most high can survive there! God is here! He sees your tears, holds your weakened body up, and is giving your mind strength now! We will walk this out together! We win! I love you!

https://youtu.be/quIMNUo8Auo[1]

---

1. Apostolicreturns, Donnie McClurkin & Marvin Winans - "STAND"

Day 88

It's a new day! You have new opportunities, new doors open, and new victories ahead! Be brand new! God has positioned you for greatness, even through your low times! Come out of your storm with fervor and aggressiveness! Win the day! And then give God the glory! You're brand new! I love you!

https://youtu.be/wehIaPYsf_Q[1]

---

1. Samuel Akerlund, Lecrae - Tell the world (lyrics)

Day 89

I love you! God bless you! Heart of God Kingdom Ministry wants to say Happy Independence Day! This our message for service today!

https://youtu.be/aBS2WzUjxqo[1]

---

1. Adrean Young, Heart of God Kingdom Ministry/Pastor Adrean

Day 90

This message is a little later than usual because I was on my knees praying for you. Yes, actually on my knees speaking the words. Why? Because the investment in making sure you are covered and blessed is important to me! How important is it to you? I can't be the only one praying for your well-being! Please take a moment and agree with me! I know you pray, but this time, I need you to say what I said for you. These words; "Lord bless their (you say my) day, their family, their jobs, their travel, their minds, their bodies, give healing, deliverance, joy, breakthrough, defend them, break the curse, renew and restore! And we will forever give you the praise, in Jesus name, Amen!" Speak it into your atmosphere! I love you!

https://youtu.be/uvcYCzMBnQA[1]

Day 91

Don't let life's circumstances make you close sighted to where you can't see God's deliverance waiting for you! Hold on! Your breakthrough, your open door, your healing, your promotion is almost here! You can make it through it! When you've done all to stand, keep standing! Jesus has your back! You don't get to fail! He has already planned your Victory party! I love you!

https://youtu.be/7tpUHbDVbpI[1]

---

1. DJ Wagner, You Can Make It : Charles Woolfork & The Praise Covenant Choir

Day 92

More love is needed now! In a time when it's easy to be divisive and trying to create more strife, God's love is the only thing that will make the difference! This doesn't mean not defending the faith or what's right. If Christ isn't seen in how it's done, then who gets the glory? Make sure His love shows through everything you do now! That will your biggest ministry! Bigger than the words you speak even! I love you!

https://youtu.be/zRfcMn1TVAM[1]

---

1. Katherinnnnne, take 6 - spread love

Day 93

I agree with you now for healing, deliverance, peace, restoration, and joy! We bind the enemy's attempts on your life and claim true victory now! The enemy can't have you or your purpose, so we lift God up now in advance for the overcoming power of the blood that covers you now! It is done! So now, let's praise him! He is worthy, and we will lift His name together! He finished it a long time ago! I love you!

https://youtu.be/5OuzCHbP4rc[1]

---

1. Jason Dennis, Lift Him Up Hezekiah Walker

Day 94

I have lost a few friends this week. It has been something that has naturally made me think about my mortality. It also allowed the Spirit of God to lead my mind to the words of my friend Pastor Tony Lee. If today was my last day, my last moments, my last breath, as much as I don't want it to be, I have to admit God has been more than good! He is my all and all, and I will praise him until my words are taken away. He has been good so worship Him! I love you!

https://youtu.be/4wq7CGGLt8I[1]

---

1. The Sanctuary PHX, Pastor Tony Lee - "If This Breath Was My Last One" 1/17/16

Day 95

Keep pressing, keep pushing, keep reaching, keep striving, keep winning, keep running, don't stop, don't turn back, you're going to make it, GOD HAS NOT FORGOTTEN YOU! Don't get discouraged. He said He would do it, so it is so! The enemy can only play with perception, but he cannot change your reality or destiny, and God has set yours along with your faith! He always has you in mind! I love you!

https://youtu.be/_OSJO4lNTFM[1]

---

1. Ny Aina Gabriella Raminosoa, GOD HAS NOT FORGOT by Tonex (Audio with lyrics)

Day 96

Your strength comes from a merciful God who has renewed his mercies for you this morning! Go into the day with the mindset you have won! You can do this! You have the strength! I love you!

https://youtu.be/FCARr6WTSFU[1]

---

1. The New Life Community Choir - Topic, Strength (Live)

Day 97

God will not fail you! Try him for real today. He will not let you down. Truly try him, which means to live like He requires, not halfway or a quarter of the way but all the way, and watch His reciprocation. The problem is that many will try to have an opinion on this but don't have any examples of a Godly lifestyle. It won't work. Live like Jesus wants you to, carry his Word in your heart and mind, love one another, and watch God answer your specifics! He is true to his promises. I love you!!

https://youtu.be/Z2wJ7vKTEmk[1]

---

1. TheMusicofthegospel, Milton Brunson There Is No Failure In God

Day 98

Tired, exhausted, and worn out, Moses wanted to keep his arms up because he k ew that along as the ones he led could see them, they would win the battle. His spirit was willing, but his flesh was weak. Aaron and Hur not only helped Moses but kept the people seeing what they needed to win! Hold someone up today! They may be tired and beaten! You don't know who all it may affect! I love you!

https://youtu.be/Bwj4J2vKUZw[1]

---

1. Rev. Milton Brunson & The Thompson Community Singers - Topic, Rest for the Weary

Day 99

E ven through our difficulties, God has still been good! A friend of mine wrote a song a few years ago that said, "If this is my last breath, I have to admit God has been so good to me regardless." That is my testimony too! Through my missteps, falls, moments of self-inflicted circumstances, God has been so good! You think about your own life and see that God has been that good! I love you!

https://youtu.be/ns4bIZ68FpE[1]

---

1. Colorado Mass Choir - Topic, So Good

Day 100

Through it all, I choose to trust Jesus! He has proven himself over and over, so why not trust Him now? Forget what you've heard and close your eyes to take away what the enemy has been trying to show you and concentrate on the memories of His grace and mercy! It will cause you to have a moment of retrospective response, and the Holy Ghost will confirm the validity of your personal history. You will want to put a praise on it! What does that mean, Preacher? This, WHEN I THINK OF THE GOODNESS OF JESUS..... I love you!

https://youtu.be/d7KdIbA2Qdw[1]

Day 101

I overslept this morning, but apparently, my body needed the rest. As I woke up to no alarm and opened my eyes, I thought about how good God's love was that I was granted one more day. His love is why I am still here. It is His love that has lifted me through many situations and circumstances! Sometimes I can't get out of my own way. But the one constant, his love still abounds! Thank God for his love this morning! I love you!

https://youtu.be/DXsJ-3_CuU8[1]

---

1. Jonathan DesVerney Gospel Channel, BeBe Winans And Bishop Marvin Winans Singing "Love Lifted Me" West Angeles COGIC HD 2018!

Day 102

Don't worry! God is on the job! All things work out for the good of them that love the Lord! Hold on to your faith, and watch your door open today! Jesus is personally seeing about you today! I'm here to remind you to go ahead and dance through this! It will confuse your haters, but it will enhance your victory! I love you!

https://youtu.be/LEarvcRRHeI[1]

---

1. Tabernacle Christian Center RTP, For My Good, Judah Band Lyrics

Day 103

In the process of restoration, the old has to be torn off and replaced! Conviction and Repentance are a part of the tearing off! Grace abounds because of our need to be redirected and restored. Don't let the enemy confuse you with guilt and shame in this time! God wants to move you into your destiny, and your foundation must be solid, which means your tear-off has to happen now! Let God restore you today! Return to the place where you could hear and see clearly! God is calling! I love you!

https://youtu.be/w8jIEoKg2R8[1]

---

1. Theverybestthereis, The Winans Restoration

Day 104

No matter what you have felt, seen, or heard, know that God is a healer! The enemy wants you to believe that the things you are facing are easily compared to other situations that were personal between God and that person. Not so! Stop listening to the "Well, Susie had the same thing, and it almost killed her" remarks! God is dealing with you personally! This is your testimony, and he is your healer! He will come through! Trust Him and believe it! I love you!

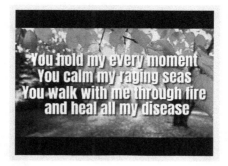

https://youtu.be/Yzejd6r9DwE[1]

Day 105

G ive God the glory today! Your awake, breathing, reading this message, able to comprehend it, God's mercy renewed, and He deserves the praise! Let your praises ring louder than the fear and complaining that is echoing in our society! He truly deserves our worship, so praise His name! I love you!

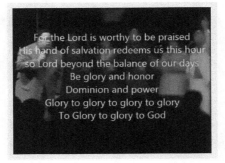

https://youtu.be/8_KpC3C25IQ[1]

---

1. Lyrics of Praise 33, "Glory to Glory to Glory" Video with Lyrics by Fred Hammond

Day 106

Get ready for your come up! They won't understand how you did it or why it's you. All you have to say is, "To God be the glory!" He is opening a door that you thought would stay closed! Time to worship equally to the blessing even before you see it! Go ahead with your victory dance! I love you!

https://youtu.be/gz6t3OIeNwA[1]

---

1. Pharrell Williams, Kim Burrell, Pharrell Williams - I See a Victory (Audio)

Day 107

God will take care of you if you trust him! He has positioned you to have His rest and love cover you. But we choose to stress and do it ourselves! He said, cast your cares on Him, but we have sleepless nights worrying about how we are going to do it. I choose to let God be God today! He will come through! I love you!

https://youtu.be/kjHo4wYgLoc[1]

---

1. CTPannell Traditional Gospel Music, Take Care Of Me with Ali Ollie Woodson - RiZen, "Live!"

Day 108

When you walk with Jesus, you have the favor of God on you! Stop killing your blessings by worrying about what someone thinks about you receiving favor! If God opens a door, gives you a promotion, or hands you something that many are trying for, give Him the glory and use it to bless someone else. Sometimes we will refuse a blessing by our own minds guilting us out of it, no more! It's yours because of favor so praise Him! I love you!

https://youtu.be/B4-fVK3cHvo[1]

---

1. Enemy of Knowing, Hezekiah Walker God Favored Me Ft Marvin Sapp And DJ Rodgers with lyricsHQ YouTube

Day 109

Today I say thanks! I am so grateful that God allowed me to still open my eyes this morning in the midst of everything. I'm going to praise Him for his mighty works and the very air that He has provided. I am thanking not for a response, although I know I can't compare to His return on high praise. My heart chooses to thank Him because he is worthy! How about you? I love you!

https://youtu.be/mLO4fbYcki4[1]

---

1. Walter Hawkins - Topic, My Gratitude

Day 110

You have been asking God, "What do I do now?" I am here to tell you this morning that He says stand still! He is about to move in your favour! It's time for your faith to meet the action, and now that you've done what He is asked you to do, He will add the increase! Now that you have done all He has told you to do; you just stand still! I love you.

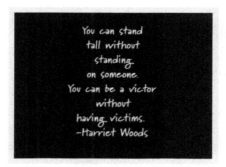

You can stand
tall without
standing
on someone.
You can be a victor
without
having victims.
—Harriet Woods

https://youtu.be/gi9rFWUPqlo[1]

---

1. WisdomTeachesme, STAND STILL! - Shirley Ceasar

Day 111

I'm in celebration today of my paren'ts' 47th wedding anniversary. I look back through the years with all of the changes, ups, downs, tough times, good times, and everything in between; there is one constant, Jesus! They kept Him as the lead, and He has blessed them and us through them! They are a true example that if Jesus is your choice, you can make it! I love them, and I love you! Hold on to Jesus! You can make it!

https://youtu.be/W5SDclTP7qg[1]

---

1. The Gospel Fill Up, We're Gonna Make It (Pt 1) - Myrna Summers & Timothy Wright

Day 112

More Jesus is what we need! He is the living Word, real love, the way, truth, and life. So, why wouldn't you want Him? The closer we get to Him, the more the cares of this world fall off of our minds. We know we are more than conquerors with Him. So why not strive for more? It's time to read more of His Word, love more, pray and fast more, and to live a life pleasing to Him. Time has wound up, and folks are going to be caught with their work undone. I love you!

https://youtu.be/iMABd4gV2gY[1]

---

1. Dave Hollister - Topic, More Of You

Day 113

As for me and my house, we will serve the Lord! Now is the time for you to make a conscious decision to go through with Jesus. Make him your lead in everything. If there is a question on whether you should align with it, use the Word to guide and not opinion and let God be the reason. God is revealing true colors and agendas in this season, and as long as Jesus is your choice, you will see favor cover you. Press toward the mark and watch Jesus show up! I love you!

https://youtu.be/CvWLnDP9-9A[1]

---

1. Cheek Life, Commissioned - I'm Going On

Day 114

G od has been faithful, and I will not take his blessings for granted. I praise him for life, health, strength, and the things I have had to go through because they have built me into the person I am. I will try not to complain! I will say thank you instead! He knows my beginning and my ending, so I must hold on to His direction so that I stay in His will. While I do that daily, I dare not complain! Can you make this your truth today? I love you!

https://youtu.be/RZ_V5Jdoy2g[1]

---

1. Gospel Tunes, "I WON'T COMPLAIN" REV.PAUL JONES (Extended Version) Praise Break

Day 115

S tay with Jesus! I promise that although you may face difficult days, His love and grace get better every day! The closer you get, the more you want of His glory! I don't need a love I can't feel, and Jesus has proven Himself to me over and over! I don't need to try any other to compare! When you've tried the best, there is no need to try the rest! He gets sweeter every day! I dare you to really try Him! You will not be disappointed! I love you!

https://youtu.be/IRbFivF9dGw[1]

---

1. Marvin Sapp, Sweeter As the Days Go By

Day 116

We serve a risen saviour, and He is our blessed hope! Try Him today! He is real, and I have the testimony to prove it! I'm sure He has done the same for you! Let the world know today that Jesus is real to you! If we lift Him, He will do the rest! Lift Him up! I love you!

https://youtu.be/2fNbahkVRcU[1]

---

1. The New Life Community Choir - Topic, Jesus Is Real (Live)

Day 117

No matter what the world or enemy has set to come against you, God is turning it around for you! Look at the finish and not the process! See where you're going, and keep your eyes on Him! New day, New mercies, New destiny, New praise! It's your day!

https://youtu.be/ZzbKwcC-Xmo[1]

---

1. Vashawnmitchell, VaShawn Mitchell - Turning Around for Me (Live)

Day 118

Prayer today, Lord, make me who I need to be for today! Tomorrow will take care of itself with your lead, so I'm focused on right now! Clean me out and replenish, restore, revive, and recharge me now! I will be successful today, I will move mountains today, do your will Lord today, give you the praise today, make a difference today, and I will win today! But it all starts with you making me over now! I already claim the victory, and my worship now is my appreciation in advance! In Jesus' name, Amen! Now run into your change! I love you!

https://youtu.be/9t6ofl39ly8[1]

---

1. Tonex - Topic, Make Me Over

Day 119

God is gonna do it! He will come through! You may not understand it right now, but God's way will be the right way for you! You will smile again! His peace is falling on you now! Hold on! I promise you; He is already moving! He said, He would. Now praise Him in advance! I love you!

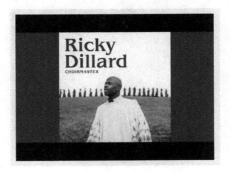

https://youtu.be/woWLdtuGkM8[1]

---

1. Rickydillardtv, God's Gonna Do It (Live)

Day 120

I f you pray, don't worry. If you worry, why pray. Don't forget that I Am has sent you! God is able to do exceedingly and abundantly above all that you can ask or think! He is able!! Stand on your prayers and work your faith! He will show up! I love you!

https://youtu.be/NBfI7hT_pYc[1]

---

1. Curlyhairdontcare07, Kirk Franklin-He's Able

Day 121

You win! Don't think any other way! The enemy wants you to see loss. When you begin to accept defeat, he will keep creating small situations that look like failures to you. That only works if he tires you out and frustrates you, but I am here to remind you that greater is He that is in you! So walk in victory today! I love you!

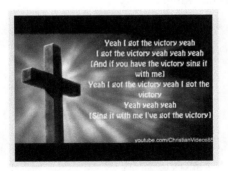

https://youtu.be/GFOUKU2djlk[1]

---

1. ChristianVideos85, Yolanda Adams - I've Got The Victory Lyrics HD

Day 122

Your praise is exactly that, YOUR praise! It's time for you to give God the praise that He's put into and developed in you! It might look different than mine. It might sound different from mine or be louder than mine or quieter than mine, but whatever it is, give it to him! He deserves it! He's bringing you out! You are now free! So worship him like your free this morning! I love you.

https://youtu.be/Y_ryOncTbBo[1]

---

1. Natalie Wilson & SOP - Topic, Free

Day 123

God is waiting to restore you! Let Him revive and replenish you. How? Give Him some you and Him time, get into your Word, pray this prayer; "Lord here I am, I give you me, now reprove and restore what I have poured out, I want to be whole again, and I praise you in advance for restoration, in Jesus name, Amen!" You can have it now! Watch how your outlook changes! I love you!

https://youtu.be/BMMA2K92M5w[1]

---

1. Tonex - Topic, Restoration

Day 124

I am so glad God gave me a chance! Even though I wasn't deserving, He made me brand new! I'm eternally grateful for His forgiveness and love! I'm so glad he deals with my mess privately! He holds me to a standard, and He constantly makes ways for me to follow! I love Him! I also love you!

https://youtu.be/xLMJ4zb9iW8[1]

---

1. Brandy Johnson, Chances by Isaac Carree

Day 125

I want to share something special that was introduced to me! This
song is a worship group singing in an African dialect. Even though
you may not understand it, you can feel his presence in the words! It is
an amazing song. Please enjoy!

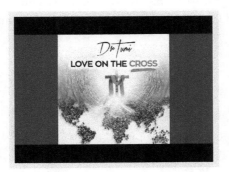

https://youtu.be/qWBOpoVMgow[1]

---

1. Dr Tumi, Ditheto (Intro)

Day 126

"...." **A**nd let the peace of God rule in your heart...." God wants to give you His peace that will keep you secure in the middle of this storm. You can not worry and know that he is handling it for you! Your body may not feel it, and your eyes might not see it, but your spirit will feel it, and you won't be afraid! The Holy Ghost inside of you will anchor you, and God's peace will hold you firm! Let him operate today! I love you!

https://youtu.be/Gb4XM7CV6Xw[1]

---

1. Donnie Nelson, Marvin Sapp - Perfect Peace

Day 127

My prayer at this time is that God finds me humble, obedient, and willing to be used. There is a need for people who can love better, serve better, pray better, and be an example and live better. I want to be in the fold. Whatever God needs, I want to be able to help. Can you pray the same? It's time for us to reach out and help others, and God will take care of you! I love you!

https://youtu.be/Clvo6rPıTYc[1]

---

1. Elvis Rigglet, Bishop Paul S. Morton Don't Do it without Me

Day 128

The prophecy over your life hasn't faded! The Word given to you hasn't changed! The times that are now are just the world answering to the consequences of sin and accepting evil. It has not detoured your calling or your destiny! Hear me, people of God. If He Said It, It Will Be So!!! Get ready for an increase in the middle of famine! Promotion in the face of layoffs! Revival in a dead environment! God is not slack in doing what He said! It's time for His glory to show in you! So what do you do now? Live well, following his Word closely! Folks will miss their chance and blessings because they have decided God's way needs to change to their way! Then they will try to blame God for not doing what he said. We aren't falling for the okeydoke! He said it, and it is so! I love you!

https://youtu.be/oTrVCZF-4pI[1]

---

1. Tribl, Man of Your Word (feat. Chandler Moore & KJ Scriven) - Maverick City | TRIBL

Day 129

Now it's time to understand your mindset for the day begins with setting the atmosphere around you. That doesn't mean you escape the battles and trials waiting for you, but it does mean your ability to dispatch those things will manifest in you quickly. Your peace and joy will remain even as the enemy tries to knock you down. Make Jesus your designated driver this morning and face the day knowing the enemy has a fight on his hands! First, thank God, then listen for His direction. Then follow His lead, and praise Him in advance for your victory! It's not always about asking or begging! Let's go! Make sure your atmosphere is set today! I love you!

https://youtu.be/3D5afHQiSo8[1]

---

1. Kurt Carr, Set the Atmosphere

Day 130

He is my God! No matter what I face, He is still God! No matter how I feel, He is still God! No matter what you say about me, He is still God! No matter where I am, He is still God! So if the constant is He doesn't change, then I can expect every miracle and victory I Have read about in the Word and seen through my life is at my access! I need Him, and I call him GOD! I love you!

God is my joy in the strength of my life beat, took away my pain and, took away my strife and, gave me a wife and, gave me a

https://youtu.be/aOYzVPJVGps[1]

---

1. Brandon Youngblood, Canton Jones G.O.D w/lyrics

Day 131

God said, "I am" when asked who He is. The answer is the ultimate covering for you! Whatever you need, desire, you are, He is! Here is today's question, when will you let him be those? It's time to let God be! Your completion and finish depend on it! I love you!

https://youtu.be/VQ-_uGePfzQ[1]

---

1. Bryce Brown, Donald Lawrence I am God

Day 132

E ven through our difficulties, God has still been good! A friend of mine wrote a song a few years ago that said if this is my last breath, I have to admit God has been so good to me regardless. That is my testimony too! Through my missteps, falls, moments of self-inflicted circumstances, God has been so good! You think about your own life and see that God has been that good! I love you!

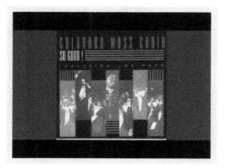

https://youtu.be/ns4bIZ68FpE[1]

---

1. Colorado Mass Choir - Topic, So Good

Day 133

Jesus made sure to show me He loved me when I felt the loneliest in my life. He wouldn't allow depression and anxiety to win, and He, through his Word, wrapped his arms around my heart and kept me through the cold of sorrow and storms of life and despair. Now I'm sharing His desire to hold you through fear and shame! You may feel like you have no one else, but He is crying out to you to try Him for real this time! When nobody else has the time or are going through themselves, He can and will be there if you look to see him! I promise you are not alone! If you want to know this for sure, contact me and let me share what he did for me! He can do the same for you! I love you!

https://youtu.be/oaUJSpqyBpI[1]

---

1. JesusFreak18102, Nobody Cared with lyrics!-Canton Jones(PLEASE COMMENT!)

Day 134

I love you! God bless you! Heart of God Kingdom Ministry wants to say Happy Independence Day! This our message for service today!

https://youtu.be/aBS2WzUjxqo[1]

---

1. Adrean Young, Heart of God Kingdom Ministry/Pastor Adrean

Day 135

You may be tired! You may be beaten! You may be weary and worn out, but I promise you right now, the very thing you have been fighting against is about to be flipped upside down and used for your advancement! God does not lose! If you walk with him, that means you do not lose! Lift a shout of praise, declaring to the world, "I AM COMING FOR MY WIN!" Take yours today! Jesus has been handing out L's to the enemy for a while now! So much that even when it looks like the enemy has won something, it still works out for my good! Praise your way into a win this day! I love you!

https://youtu.be/3TOPBr8k8xY[1]

1. Elevation Worship, Never Lost feat. Tauren Wells | Live | Elevation Worship

Day 136

"Real love," a phrase that many search a lifetime for, is in your reach! Know God, know love! No God, no love! He is waiting for you to experience Him so he can show you what love is! Will today be the day you find it? I love you!

https://youtu.be/mooa3-QJhL4[1]

---

1. M Brown, John P. Kee-I Want To Love You

Day 137

The joy in Jesus is what gives you strength. If you want more strength, concentrate on finding more joy in Him. We tend to see more of ourselves and our problems when we feel weak, sad, and depressed. That's because the enemy knows that the way to cut our strength from us is to block our view of Jesus. Look past what others have done, what life has presented, what you have failed at, and find the Saviour who is waiting to erase the condemnation of those things and grant you grace and mercy which will return your joy. He is waiting for you! I love you!

https://youtu.be/Mq6hprGOxpY[1]

1. Gaither Music TV, Richard Smallwood - The Center Of My Joy (Live)

Day 138

I t's gonna be alright! Don't wait to see it. Go ahead and praise now! God is on the job! You may not see it yet, but I was told to tell you that sometimes it is necessary to worship the same amount as your request to press your faith into motion! What does that mean? Large request equals large praise! I asked for something huge, so I'm going to praise him huge now! How about you? I know it's already alright! I love you!

https://youtu.be/a-eYPxOBv4E[1]

---

1. Vivian White, Alright by Fred Hammond

Day 139

I dare you to trust Him! He is waiting to prove your faith! It's time to let your faith overcome your fear! He hasn't given you the fear, and there is no fear in Him! He waits to push you through! So trust Him today! I love you!

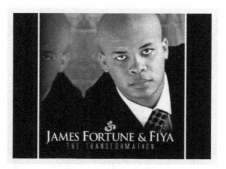

https://youtu.be/rRwQy2eQbJM[1]

---

1. GospelMusicTV, James Fortune & FIYA - I Trust You

Day 140

J esus wants you! You are special, and you are more than a needy job to him. You have been made perfect! He knew you before you were formed in the womb, and he molded your destiny in His hands before you were a name given in a nursery! An enemy and a dying world have told you that you are only worth what you last failed at, but Jesus says your life is worth the blood that He exchanged for it! Where you are right now, in your thoughts and tears, know that I was told to remind you this morning that you are wanted! He wants you! He loves you, and so do I! Let Him hold you today! His spirit longs to show you!

https://youtu.be/IMDQtf-PT24[1]

1. Unite With Jesus! Lyrics, Wanted-Danny Gokey-(LYRICs)

Day 141

Give God real praise today! Take a minute to separate yourself from tradition, "normal," the same old same old. Strip away the cares, worries, and troubles and let your mind stand bare before him so your praise will continue unhindered and pure! Then tell God who you are and why you're praising Him! It will change your relationship! Imagine the person you are in love with, standing in front of you, bearing their souls' love for you for no other reason but to let you know! That's how God will feel about it, and the response will be life-altering, I promise! He deserves complete praise from us, so it's time!

https://youtu.be/moXYg7SzClQ[1]

1. LifeInToday MediaGroup, B Slade Total Praise

Day 142

He is still a healer! God is still delivering! He is still making a way! He has been riding in your ship in the storm, waiting for you to ask him to calm your winds and waves! He will pull you through! He will not fail you! He just needs you to do more than saying you're giving it all to him! Get out of the way! He has your back! I promise! I love you!

https://youtu.be/YYFqjGEuTh4[1]

---

1. Christopher Walker, Jermaine Dolly - Pull Us Through

Day 143

Put your trust in Him! Activate your faith! Time to do what you talk about! Put all of your cares on Jesus! He said he cares for the birds, which are not nearly as important as you are to him, so don't worry! He will be there for you! He is there now! Trust it! I love you!

https://youtu.be/ZyB8fv_CJfI[1]

---

1. Slaychelle, The Clark Sisters - "Cast Your Cares On Him"

Day 144

When you look in the mirror, who do you see? Better yet, who will everyone else see? We reflect who we live for and who we represent, so if the Jesus you say you serve isn't in that reflection, it's time to identify who is. If you choose not to be that reflection, I am not talking to you. But if you say for Christ I live and for Christ I day, what are you reflecting? Now pray, meditate, and look again! It may change your morning! I love you!

https://youtu.be/dhfFsj5ALNo[1]

---

1. YourMowf, Anointed - It's not the I but the You in Me

Day 145

It will be yours! God has designed such a time as this to continue to prove he is God, and his people will continue to be blessed! Your blessings, promotions, healing, breakthrough, opened doors, and revival will still be had if you hold on and believe! Don't doubt him! He said, ask in His name and watch him work! But remember, staying in the will of God means to remain in the way God designed, not your way! I love you!

https://youtu.be/m_gE-rEH96E[1]

---

1. Robbieatnsudotcom, It Is For Me by the Miami Mass Choir

Day 146

Through it all, I have learned to seek Jesus until he takes away all pain, strife, uncertainty, and problems. We may find ourselves in a place of tears, but I promise you he is waiting to pay you for every ounce of pain in each one! Take courage in knowing that He is a covering for you, and He will hide you when you need rest if you fully seek Him! I love you!

https://youtu.be/QKyfI_oBCpI[1]

---

1. William Becton - Topic, 'Til You Take the Pain Away

Day 147

And the Lord said, "Behold, they are one people, and they have all one language, and this is only the beginning of what they will do. And nothing that they propose to do will now be impossible for them.

Genesis 11:6 ESV

GOD HIMSELF SAID that if a people were unified and spoke the same language (means all in agreement thought, mind, spirit, and goals too), there was nothing they couldn't do right or wrong. Do you think we should finally do what he empowered us to? Unity is the only way we make a change! I love you!

https://youtu.be/ZypKcB-w5VY[1]

---

1. Praise shark, We Will Stand

Day 148

He wants you! All of you! Not half or some but all! Let the redeemed of the Lord say so! Let us be a light to a flailing world, and let love be our guide! He will deliver if we allow Him to be our all! Taste and see that He is good! I love you!

https://youtu.be/-QsG5DwbAvQ[1]

---

1. New Manna Community Church, He Wants It All by Forever Jones

Day 149

L et the Joy of the Lord be your strength! You will make it! You will survive! You will win! You are exactly where God needs you to be! Realize that he has positioned and ordained this time for your come up! I love you!

https://youtu.be/I_uoOY-x_dw[1]

---

1. The7Meek, My Joy (with lyrics)

Day 150

If your reading this message, you have been given the greatest blessing possible, another day to live out your purpose! Do you know how blessed you are? In spite of all you see ahead, the fact you can see it still means that God has a way for you to make it through it! You're more blessed than you realize! Now praise Him for the opportunity, and let's go get it! I love you!

https://youtu.be/Q2a63LohEkI[1]

---

1. Denzeldavon2, Fred Hammond & R.F.C | We're Blessed

Day 151

B e free! Leave your burdens and cares at the feet of Jesus and walk in freedom today! Let him give you peace! It can be yours if you would only trust Him and step out of your own way! Grab it and keep it! It feels good to be free! I love you!

https://youtu.be/onoC8KAENSw[1]

---

1. Millennial Hardware, Freedom- Eddie James lyrics video

Day 152

In honor of mothers, today we would like to take time to say we love you! Both to the ones we can hold, and in memory of those that God has allowed to have their rest and reward, we love you! Even from the cross, Jesus took time to make sure his mother was taken care of. I have a loving, beautiful warrior woman for a mom. It's her fault I'm overweight because she cooks too good. I was spoiled (not as much as my brother and sister, though, lol), and her prayers covered me when I didn't know how to cover myself. So I say this, "Momma, I love and appreciate you!" Please make sure you tell her today! And I understand if it's a hard day today. Still, I encourage you to take a moment to appreciate the memories of a mother who was an angel then and now! I love you!

https://youtu.be/vli-jCvUalw[1]

---

1. Vickie Finans - Topic, You're More Than a Mom (A Tribute Feat. Marvin Winans, Jr.)

Day 153

The battle seems so much easier when you realize you're not alone! The enemy wants you to believe he has isolated you like a pack of hunting lionesses and has you surrounded, ready for the kill. Jesus said, "I'm never going to leave you! No matter where you find yourself, I am there!" Perk up this morning! Set your feet in the ground, straighten up your back, and get ready to start swinging but realize you may not even see the action because your battles are His too! He will get it in for you and leave you to pick up the spoils as you walk through the defeated adversary! Your never alone y'all! I love you!

https://youtu.be/srGIp4LO-XM[1]

1. Tori Kelly, Tori Kelly - Never Alone (Official Live Video)

Day 154

I have joy because Jesus is my focus! He is my reason for success and survival, and I will praise His name forever! He will deliver for you if you focus on Him! I love you!

https://youtu.be/Mq6hprGOxpY[1]

---

1. Gaither Music TV, Richard Smallwood - The Center Of My Joy (Live)

Day 155

When the unity of all people is necessary to have the strength to make a change, we see more separation and anger instead. The enemy has effectively created a climate that makes wrongdoing explainable and right actions unpopular. God's people are silently stuck in between. We know the prophecy of God's Word and know our place in it, but to overcome, we must seek God and come together! All of God's children! This has to go beyond political alignment and personal taste! If we are who we say we are, we have to be sure that all children are in a world where it's safe for them to go to school and make it home. God's people, all people together, can make a change! I love you!

https://youtu.be/NIBx8ZbLMuk[1]

---

1. Gospel Nostalgia, "Overcome" (1982) D. J. Rogers

Day 156

On this Father's day, some may not feel the joy that everyone else is experiencing due to circumstances or loss. Still, I want to encourage you with this; God said he would always be there, and he is the first and greatest Father! By faith, we know he has and will fill in the gaps for you! Just trust him! He said he would, and I believe him! I love you!

https://youtu.be/DLlnPjXNaWg[1]

---

1. Rheem1975, King James Version - God Will See You Through.wmv

Day 157

We serve an awesome Saviour! Giver of life, health, strength, hope, love, and freedom! Every day I will praise him! We aren't worthy of it, but he has made us so! His grace and mercy are enough to praise him for today! Take some time to thank Him! I love you!

https://youtu.be/d_UE7xgNOzM[1]

---

1. Canton Jones, Charles Jenkins AWESOME REMIX ft. Jessica Reedy, Isaac Carree, Da' T.R.U.T.H. & @CantonJones

Day 158

This morning, God only said a short phrase to me; "You Will Win!"
So stand on it and have a beautiful day! I love you!

https://youtu.be/KjkqPDv_Xgg[1]

---

1. Cheek Life, Commissioned - Victory

Day 159

S peak your reality now and then walk it like you talk it! Let your faith direct your feet and believe the promises of God! Even in this time, God is still God! Its morning! Some of you have endured weeping, so come out of it and receive your joy! Jesus is meeting you at your need today! I love you!

https://youtu.be/jZjKıEJcbys[1]

---

1. Eydely WoshipLivingGod, BLESSINGS ON BLESSINGS ANTHONY BROWN & GROUP THERAPY By EydelyWorshipLivingGodChannel

Day 160

I s there still a praise on your lips? Have you purposed a moment of worship in the middle of this storm? Can your anger, hurt, despair, or pain allow a Hallelujah anyhow? It's time to be who we said we are and act like we said we would act when the days were sunnier and not so dark! God is still God, and his prophecies are still being fulfilled, so I say Hallelujah anyhow! Yes, I will still support and march in protest peacefully and let the world know that change is needed, but there is a priority in me to praise God first for who he was, is, and yet to be in my life! Find your Hallelujah this morning and give it to Him! I love you!

https://youtu.be/hR3Uqc2SSmc[1]

1. Thomas Whitfield - Topic, Hallelujah Anyhow

Day 161

I don't care what it looks like! I don't care what you've heard! Jesus never fails! You will win because if He is for you, He is more than the world against you! If you haven't tried Him, you don't know what true victory feels like! He is enough! I love you!

https://youtu.be/4t7T5KTaHG8[1]

---

1. Gilbertmonk, Lowell Pye - Jesus Never Fails

Day 162

Today's prayer is for God's awesome presence to fill our hearts and produce an overflow of his power. Making all of us feel his rain on us and giving us the ability to walk through this day in purpose! His will and his way even right now! Pour it out on us, Lord! I love you!

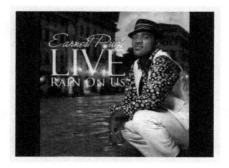

https://youtu.be/iJncObqrJR8[1]

---

1. GospelMusicTV, Earnest Pugh - Rain On Us

Day 163

When you're in a fight, you have two choices, win or lose. It's time to win! It's time to realize that the enemy we're fighting against only has one thing on his mind, to kill us! So it's time to fight like we're being fought! I don't care if your enemy has their feelings hurt or doesn't like what I'm saying! You win today! You overcome today! You become free today! You are healed today! It's time to win your fight and let Jesus give you the strength to be Victorious! I love you!

https://youtu.be/6JLbsGgfpO4[1]

---

1. Tony Lee - Topic, The Devil Don't Like This

Day 164

My moment of transparent worship this morning, Lord, you are my everything! I can't move without you, can't live without you, can't breathe without you! I will hide in you! Today and forever will I remain chasing your will and way, and because of your Holy Ghost, I can abide there! I worship you with my whole heart Jesus! Now those who are reading this and listening to this, We on one accord, change the atmosphere around us! We declare change and deliverance never seen before, even now! This is my prayer, and I will forever give you the praise, Jesus! I love you!

https://youtu.be/OAXXEdVhH8w[1]

1. Gardenboy32, TONY LEE AND UNITY LIVE

Day 165

Run into your destiny today! Seize the day! God gave it to you, so take it! Nothing can stop or change what God promised you except you! No more fear and procrastination! It's always been yours, but now it is time for you to be vigilant and focused and let God's purpose in you manifest itself! Get it! I love you!

https://youtu.be/ohbYXWhsguA[1]

---

1. Pastor Mike Jr. - Topic, Big Extended Version

Day 166

I remember when our musicians would miss the service. We wouldn't have sticks for the drums at service when I was a kid, and the children would get the bongos and tambourines. My father would have that metal ball shaker, and the Pastor had an old set of cymbals. The church would erupt in worship so high we would end up praying for God to give us added rest because we would get out so late! What's the point? It wasn't the music that made us praise so hard! It was the goodness of a risen saviour who, despite what we saw, was working it out by our faith, and we praised him for it! How about you this morning? Is it the music or Jesus that has your worship and praise moving? I love you!

https://youtu.be/zI1O9cvdIKs[1]

---

1. Mali Music, No Muzick

Day 167

Give it all to Him! No more trying it your way! God's will cannot be done your way! It has to be directed by Him! We often wonder why the way we have gone has been extra difficult, but we should check ourselves and see if we even asked God if we should go that way. Surrender everything to not only the will of God but also the way of God! I love you!

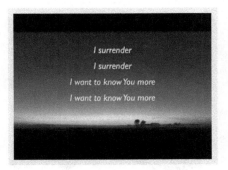

https://youtu.be/jgsqfjRslzA[1]

---

1. Gary McDuffee, Hillsong - I Surrender (with lyrics)

Day 168

We will come through as pure gold! Nothing that comes through fire remains the same. Even if the change is minimal, fire proves it! Beloved, we are being shaped and molded, and we will be changed! We must stay focused on the Way of God, which puts us into God's will and allows us to stay in the path that God has set for us! If we can do this, our change will come. Don't be consumed or burnt up! Press through, believe, unite, and let's make it together! I love you!

https://youtu.be/3Ea6BPW8GI8[1]

---

1. Praise and Worship, "We're Gonna Make It" Myrna Summers & Timothy Wright lyrics

Day 169

J esus is ready to heal your brokenness! He is waiting for you to leave it at his feet. Stop trying to do it yourself! He can complete you and take a heart and mend it like no one else can! Are you tired of being broken? It's your time, and this day is your moment! He will do it for you! Give him a chance for real this time! I love you!

https://youtu.be/aM_IHQ4pfhw[1]

---

1. Keith Malveaux, Broken Don't Pass Me By - Indiana Bible College IBC

Day 170

"I'm sorry" is a phrase that has been reduced to a pickup line or a point of manipulation. Its sincerity has stopped mostly when it includes saying it to someone we feel has wronged us. It is said so that we can move on and not to exhibit love. If asking for forgiveness isn't followed immediately by change, it meant nothing! Which leads us to be forgiven by our Heavenly father. "He knows my heart" is often said to defend our missteps but should be realized in our everyday life! Lord Forgive me being said without change means, exactly! He knows your heart! I love you!

https://youtu.be/DhMro_PnJXg[1]

1. Emmanuel Jones, "Forgive Me" - Timothy Wright & The Concert Choir

Day 171

In spite of everything going on, my answer to Jesus is still Yes! I will do what he says! I will follow his word! Let's follow him today! I love you!

https://youtu.be/Kerg9Y9USRU[1]

---

1. Malacomg, Rev. James Moore - Yes Lord

Day 172

You are worth the trouble! You are what all the fuss is about! You are precious in his sight! He made you from a design and thought from his mind! Just the way you are and on purpose for his purpose! Believe it! You are fearfully and wonderfully made! Now go out and be great because you were built for this! I love you!

https://youtu.be/va5I6MOF-8M[1]

---

1. Mack Simpson Music Ministry, Anthony Brown & group therAPy - Trust In You (LYRICS)

Day 173

R eturn to prayer! God needs some time with you! When you need relief, breakthrough, healing, deliverance, a way out of no way, or your peace restored, he is only a prayer away! He is waiting for you to step out of the way so he can get in the way of the things you're going through. Try going to sleep in prayer! You wake up with answers! Give him more than 1 min and 30 seconds and try listening instead of talking the whole time! It will change your days, I promise! I love you!

https://youtu.be/Gjfs3rSIpIQ[1]

---

1. Sounds of Blackness - Topic, The Pressure Pt. 1

Day 174

I t's time to show love! There is so much loss and grieving in the world, and the enemy has convinced many that he is winning, but I know that God's love wins! We must spread it to a dying world and a wounded people! How? By meeting them at their need. I challenge you to help someone today! Yes, you can help more than one person, but let's concentrate on at least one person a day. That's a beginning, and everyone does it. We will promote change by love! If you can't love, then you don't know God! That's the word! I love you!

https://youtu.be/zRfcMnrTVAM[1]

---

1. @take6official, #spreadlove2020challenge

Day 175

The same God in the beginning who conquered everything that his people needed him to is the same God who is in your corner this morning! Take advantage of it! If God is for you, he is more than the world against you! You can overcome what you're walking into! And like back then, the journey may not be the route you envisioned, but his grace and mercy back his way! Trust him and keep pressing! I love you!

https://youtu.be/VQ-_uGePfzQ[1]

---

1. Bryce Brown, Donald Lawrence I am God

Day 176

G od knows! He reads tears, and he feels your hurts! You don't have to say a word! Sometimes a wave of your hand can begin the healing process because God understands! You don't have to find the perfect words! Just wave it away! I love you!

https://youtu.be/E7UsCqNDdxg[1]

---

1. The New Life Community Choir - Topic, Wave It Away

Day 177

You are still in the fight! It doesn't matter that it looks like your down on the judge's scorecards. You're about to win by knock out! It was never a question! Now you will come through this on top! God said, "There is nothing impossible in me!" Now grab hold of the vision and come out swinging! It is not time to sit back and survive! It's time to get the Victory! Whatever you desire from God, don't just ask! Go Get It! I love you!

https://youtu.be/aO9qJpX_BVc[1]

---

1. Mizzpinkc, It's Not Over (When God Is in It) feat. James Fortune & Jason Nelson

Day 178

You can face today and win! Even when days are heavy, and it seems like the day before was a loss, your Saviour has a blessing for you today, and it begins with the fact that your reading this message! His new mercy this morning has allowed us to be positioned right where we need to be for us to win! He keeps getting better to us as the days go by! You may not understand the route your taking but believe in the destination! Have a wonderful, prosperous day! I love you!

https://youtu.be/IRbFivF9dGw[1]

---

1. Marvin Sapp, Sweeter As the Days Go By

Day 179

You may be in a place where people surround you but still lonely or have a lot but feel like you are still missing everything. God wants you to know that Him being the "I Am" means if you give Jesus a try, He will never leave you lonely, and he will complete you, so you are satisfied! You have been positioned through your process for God to show himself strong to you! Yes, you! Personally! He will not fail you though you feel like you have failed! Trust him today and watch your forever change! I love you!

https://youtu.be/-bk5iRcphWY[1]

1. Josh Lopez, Josh Lopez & Mark Townsend- God you are God performed by Lisa Lopez and the CBC Choir

Day 180

L ate last night, as I was going to sleep, the enemy tried to attack my mind. My peace was disturbed, but before I could react, my daughter sent me a text that said, "Something told me to text you and say, You've got the victory!" Yes, you probably would have reacted as I did! Even when you're under attack and think you are alone, Jesus finds a way to reach your mind! Just expect it instead of doubting it! Be encouraged! He will never leave you! I love you!

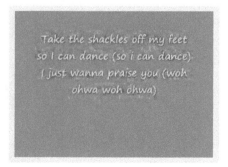

Take the shackles off my feet
so I can dance (so i can dance)
I just wanna praise you (woh
ohwa woh ohwa)

https://youtu.be/4PfuT-oYAf4[1]

---

1. Judy G, Shackles (praise you) by MARY MARY (lyrics)

Day 181

One of my former Pastors used to pray a benediction that said, "Watch and pray, stay peaceful, and give no place to the Devil, in Jesus name, Amen." I used to think, "Why would anyone give the devil a place?" not realizing how easily this happens if you're not in a 1 Thessalonians 5:17 state of mind! Sometimes our daily walk requires us to physically change our routine to escape from the very things we complain are hindering us! Well, I declare this morning that I am shaking off those things and that God looses here on earth, me from the desires, thoughts, and habits that put me in an open arms situation to the plans and devices of the devil! Shake yourself like Sampson and feel the ropes, vines, or chains of oppression fall off this morning! I love you!

https://youtu.be/FfUZXoMDmrU[1]

---

1. Snitsny, Vickie Winans - Shake Yourself Loose

Day 182

The Holy Spirit seeks to encourage you! Even in a time like this! He has covered you to give you rest and to let your heart be strengthened! You have the power to stand today because He has established new ability in you! Now stand! It doesn't matter how yesterday ended or what you dreamed last night! It's about what you have been empowered to do right now! Be encouraged! I love you!

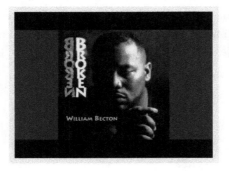

https://youtu.be/D8rFU8Ze8G4[1]

---

1. William Becton - Topic, Be Encouraged

Day 183

We must always remember this; your life tells the truth! It doesn't matter who, what, or how you say you are. If your life doesn't back it up, you are not credible or believable! You can scream it at the top of your lungs and make billboards about it, but if it isn't in sync with your living, you are lying to yourself and the world! Every step of a righteous person is directed, ordered, set up, and prepared by God! Yes, the difficult times too! They come to make you strong! When your patience has run out, you're tired, or you feel backed into a corner, I challenge you to take a deep breath, refocus, and find the footprints you need to follow! Jesus already walked them out for you. Just walk in them! I love you!

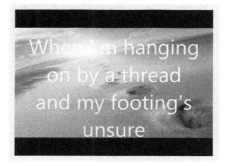

When I'm hanging
on by a thread
and my footing's
unsure

https://youtu.be/sx76I9acTrQ[1]

---

1. WordLife TV, Your Steps are Ordered Lyric Video

Day 184

In a place of awe and worship this morning! During all the news that's not news, rumors, and panic going on, making it difficult to know what to believe and what not to, God has still been there. Difficult times come to make us strong! So we offer up praise to Him that healeth us! He deserves our praise! Though there are still some dark days ahead, I will not concentrate on the storm but continue to look at the Son shining through the clouds! He deserves your worship today! I love you!

https://youtu.be/NTLzYDRoOxs[1]

---

1. InsideTheGospel, You Deserve By Chrystal Rucker

Day 185

Through everything you may be facing this morning, I'm here to tell you Jesus still loves you! You are in His heart, and He wants what's best for you! Troubles don't ever mean his love is absent, but the opposite! It takes more to love someone at tough times and stress when they are hard to love, but He loves you anyway! Feel His love today and let it help you pull through! I love you too!

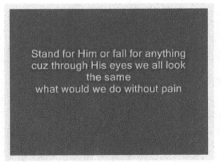

Stand for Him or fall for anything
cuz through His eyes we all look
the same
what would we do without pain

https://youtu.be/uIDZmXb-r7Q[1]

---

1. OzarkTiger076, Fighting Temptations He Still Loves Me Lyrics

Day 186

W hat's best for us is the will of God but understanding that takes the love of God. When we go through tough times, it takes God's love and understanding to help us to see that every happening isn't about us even though it might affect us. The loss of a loved one, the changing of a friendship, the difficult moments in life are often about God's will for others also. We must seek God for both strength and understanding to know that his will is what's best for us, and we will praise him in the midst of it! I love you!

https://youtu.be/1qxsosfURZM[1]

---

1. GospelMusicTV, Your Will - Darius Brooks

Day 187

You don't have to look any further! Jesus is exactly what you are looking for! Often imitated but never duplicated, and He is all you need! Through storms and tough times, He will be there! Try Him if you haven't! Remember Him if you know Him! He is waiting for you to say, "I'm yours!" I love you!

https://youtu.be/RzoiJKJtbUY[1]

---

1. Robbieatnsudotcom, Whatcha Lookin 4 by Kirk Franklin and the Family

Day 188

When God is in it, everything changes! When His presence is felt, we even feel better! So if that is the case, why do we leave or do things to move out His presence? He made it clear he will not leave us, so it is we who move out of place! Your challenge today is to keep your building (body) one that God will stay in all day and watch your situation change all day! I love you!

https://youtu.be/8kidyx9Igj4[1]

Day 189

I t will be yours! God has designed such a time to continue to prove he is God, and his people will continue to be blessed! Your blessings, promotions, healing, breakthrough, opened doors, and revival will still be had if you hold on and believe! Don't doubt him! He said, ask in His name and watch him work! But remember, staying in the will of God means to remain in the way God designed, not your way! I love you!

https://youtu.be/m_gE-rEH96E[1]

---

1. Robbieatnsudotcom, It Is For Me by the Miami Mass Choir

Day 190

Sometimes we find ourselves just talking and venting and then call it prayer time. We are in a season of listening! When was the last time we went to God and said, "You speak, Lord!" And we just listened and absorbed him? Right now, Lord, we need a word from you, what, when, where, and how? Lead Lord, and we will trust your way! We will forever give you the praise! In Jesus' name... I love you!

https://youtu.be/pI8AQAoi6F8[1]

---

1. Miketodd8, waiting to hear from you

Day 191

We have been blessed! Even if it isn't openly apparent. We are searching for a blessing in a time of hardship, but many have socially distanced themselves from God. The praying, reading, and worship have been replaced because of a dependency on a building to provide the motivation to do them. Yet, we find ourselves blessed. We serve a savior who has met us at our need, and even though our promises have been slack, he blesses anyway. This may not be your message this morning, and if not, Keep On Keeping on! But if you have fallen back from your regular relationship with Jesus, he needs you back. I love you!

https://youtu.be/xXjyuNBWujM[1]

---

1. RachaelLampaVideos, Rachael Lampa - Blessed - acoustic performance (@rachaellampa)

Day 192

Your circumstances cannot change your purpose! Good, bad, or in between, always have a humble servant's heart and keep helping each other! If we can do this, the overflow of God's grace will continue to cover you! Make giving your priority and watch the reciprocation that comes from God! Always serve God, and he will beat your efforts in return! I love you!

https://youtu.be/M_ak-4SQ_FE[1]

---

1. Jerome Hunt, Jermaine Dolly Serve Offical Video

Day 193

Have you prayed? If so, why are you worried? Giving it to God means exactly that. Out of your hands and into his! He has got you, and he knows what you need to go with it! Make sure you know who you are! The prayers of the righteous... Righteous doesn't only mean right living but right believing also! I love you!

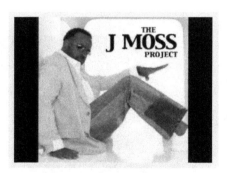

https://youtu.be/LMwcoMYVVA4[1]

---

1. Maurie McDonald, J Moss-Don't Pray & Worry

Day 194

Your plans only work if your steps are ordered! You may think you're going somewhere, but the will of God has a way of bringing you back to where you were supposed to go, so why not be led there the first time? Give your way to him now, and he will lead you through this valley of the shadow of death! You don't have to fear because he said he would never leave you! His presence will make you feel his strength through you, I promise! I love you!

https://youtu.be/Y4D-EAU6AZQ[1]

---

1. Alphaape1, Pastor Marvin Winans sings Wherever I go

Day 195

It's being worked out now! You have prayed on it, and now it's time to let Jesus handle it! Go ahead and let your faith work! It's going to be alright! There is no problem that He can't fix! It will be ok! I'm standing with you! I love you!

https://youtu.be/tHvbhN1E3ng[1]

---

1. Change Is Coming, BeBe & CeCe Winans: "It's OK" Lyrics

Day 196

Don't depend on your eyes and ears to see God's glory in this season! He is here in the middle of all the chaos, but the enemy is stirring up the fog and smoke to keep you from seeing, and the thunder is keeping you from hearing Him. So do what works best, be patient, and praise Him anyway! Your patience proves your confidence in Jesus. Adding your increase and your praise confirms you hear your victory! Beloved, we are in a confusing moment, but God's peace that passeth all understanding shall guard your heart and mind through Christ Jesus! I love you!

https://youtu.be/po_44oy_TSs[1]

1. Fred Jerkins - Topic, Patiently Praising (feat. Lowell Pye)

Day 197

The same Jesus that delivered me years ago will be my trust now! He has not changed, and by the word of my testimony and the blood that was shed for me, I will not fear! I just praise him now! He deserves the highest praise! What will you do in the midst of chaos? It's time to give him control! I love you!

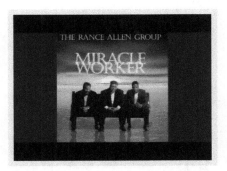

https://youtu.be/jvA-DU1okEc[1]

---

1. Willie Ellebie Gospel Channel, He Delivered Me - The Rance Allen Group

Day 198

Why is it important for us to live Holy? Because Jesus can't dwell in a house that isn't! If we are indeed the church and we have cried out for so long for no more church, as usual, it's time to take this opportunity to show the world who the church really is! It isn't the building or the place! It is us, but if your looking for the Lord, the church must be Holy! I love you!

https://youtu.be/fWjMKrYpyIQ[1]

---

1. The Young and the Redeemed, "The Holy Place" (2000) Ricky Dillard & New G

Day 199

What do you see? Can you see your change coming? You have prayed your prayer, and now it is time to stand on your faith! Hold on to it! God has heard you, and you may not understand the journey, but the destination is exactly where you are supposed to be! So keep holding on and keep on keeping on! I love you!

https://youtu.be/V24-3bS0a2I[1]

---

1. AndyMatch, Sounds Of Blackness - Hold On (Change Is Comin') (Roger Troutman's Remix)

Day 200

Is Jesus enough for you? If you don't get the riches or fame you dreamt about, is He enough? It's easy to say yes when you pose the question that way, but what if the question was simplified? Like this; What if the answer to your last prayer is no? What if His grace has to be sufficient for you through your suffering? What if you feel your mind attacking itself and you hear the voices that urge you to take other routes of relief? Is He enough? Now is the time to fall back on the years of Sunday school lessons and Bible studies to find his voice deep inside you telling you through his own words, "I am enough for you!" When you can stand on Him, his promises, and the peace he brings will satisfy you! Stand on him today! Know Him, learn of Him, Talk to Him! I love you!

https://youtu.be/EPXT78ueoqI[1]

---

1. Whatisthepoint, the walls group satisfied lyrics

Day 201

You still win today! Get up and go get it! Greater is he that is in you than he that is attacking the world and has caused panic! Refuse to stop swinging and fight out of the corner! You can't lose! The Savior has prepared you and has been watching for his chance to double team your adversaries! You win, and it starts with today! I love you!

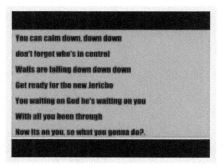

https://youtu.be/4alkB5yyw9o[1]

---

1. Lyrics World, Kirk Franklin- 123 Victory Lyrics!!!

Day 202

It's going to be alright! Your storm is ending! We are coming out! God wants you to know that your dawn is coming and midnight is over! So stay the course and keep holding on! I love you!

https://youtu.be/kW-12AkEAyg[1]

---

1. 1blessedladie, Be Encouraged by William Becton & Friends

Day 203

It has now been a little over a year since I started sending morning inspirations, and it has really blessed me as much as it has blessed you. Now is a time of refreshing and recharge, so this will be the last one for a bit, but it's not over! I want to leave this as I take a break though, you had the strength all along! It's time for you to look in the mirror and see the child of the King that you are and encourage yourself. Jesus is there in you, and this is another Victory taking place for you! I love you!

https://youtu.be/rFNHmA9a2gI[1]

---

1. GospelMusicTV, Encourage Yourself By: Donald Lawrence

Day 204

I began to look at the numbers of the estimates and the results according to the experts, and I heard God say, "Did you hear my results yet?" I had let the news and internet begin to grow my narrative. I almost forgot how God always moves in the middle of the storm! That doesn't mean I stop listening to safety and common sense, but it means I will trust God over man! Time to let go and let God! How about you? I love you!

https://youtu.be/YugivPgi2Fc[1]

---

1. Marten Frankel, Bishop Paul S. Morton & PJ - Let Go, Let God

Day 205

I t's time for us to realize that settling for anything less than extraordinary love in our lives is a disservice to ourselves. We serve a God who has proven that love can be forgiving, healing, mending, perfect, joyful, intimate, comforting, completing, protecting, humbling, and exciting. Still, we will accept less than all of these and wonder why we feel like we do. How do we get it? By learning to love ourselves with all of these attributes and letting God love us the same. That creates a heart like His, which allows you to love somebody else the same way! I LOVE YOU!

https://youtu.be/g7uxSXGsTbY[1]

1. Isaac Carree, Ordinary Just Won't Do

Day 206

Today is a day of praise in the midst of our coming out! Yes, the pandemic is still active. Yes, we are still following social rules to ensure others' safety. However, we still abide by telling someone why we are concerned but not afraid! I have a friend named Jesus who assures me I'm ok! He deserves the praise because although others want to have the credit, he makes a way to provide for you every time! If you wait on Him, He comes through! Tell someone today that Jesus is still delivering, and he gets the praise! I love you!

https://youtu.be/MGDUP4KlSPg[1]

---

1. JermaineDollyEVO, Jermaine Dolly - You (Official Video)

Day 207

No matter where I am now, I can see where God has brought me from when I look back! You don't have to understand my praise or tears but know this, if you had been standing in my place just a while ago, you would feel like praising Him too! Corona has nothing on where many of you have been through already, so praise him with me today! He deserves it! I love you!

https://youtu.be/7eZoVI9OeRs[1]

---

1. Allen Freeman, Donnie McClurkin -Thank You Jesus

Day 208

Where are your feet grounded? As for me and my house.....! We are standing on the promises of Jesus Christ, our saviour! It doesn't matter what it looks like or what the numbers say! On Christ, the solid rock we stand! Make sure your foundation is on the rock, and I am not talking about Prudential! I love you!

https://youtu.be/LIıKpyoN-4Y[1]

---

1. Kadeem Graves, Solid Rock - Walter Hawkins and The Love Center Choir

Day 209

We have an incredible God who has enough mercy to cover in the time of despair but must stay true to his word and fulfill the Word's prophecies. What does that mean? Make Jesus your choice while you have time; love everybody as he does you. Understand that Holiness is more than memorizing verses and good lines, strive every day to accomplish the purpose He has created you for, and never let fear guide your living! This world is crying out for you to do what God has made you for! If you don't know what that is, I dare you to stop talking for a minute and listen to hear Him tell you. He is awesome enough to not only tell you but to provide everything you need to do it! I love you!

https://youtu.be/d_UE7xgNOzM[1]

---

1. Canton Jones, Charles Jenkins AWESOME REMIX ft. Jessica Reedy, Isaac Carree, Da' T.R.U.T.H. & @CantonJones

Day 210

If I came to your door and knocked over and over and then when you opened the door I stood there and wouldn't come in, how would you feel? I know how I would react. Well, why do we do God that way? We pray for doors to be open, a way out, and relief, but when he opens the door, we stand there, not moving! I hear someone thinking, "I need to make sure it's Him!" My answer is this, if you knocked on my door and I answered, who else would it be? Plus, spirit knows spirit! If you can't recognize him, then that's another message for another day! See the door open, run through it! He has answered you! I love you!

https://youtu.be/fWhoQjoFz4M[1]

1. Stephan, Maranda Curtis - "Way Maker"

Day 211

It's ok! Your going to make it! Just make sure you proclaim the name Jesus and watch your difficulties spread away like pouring Dawn soap into greasy water! His name carries power, and you can wield it like a battle axe! He is waiting to hear it called so he can show up for you! Stop calling your own number and let him do what he said! It's time to let Him be who you sing about! I love you!

https://youtu.be/xlSZh-wsW6w[1]

---

1. Kirk Franklin, Something About The Name Jesus Pt. 2

Day 212

G od said He is the one that heals Us! Have we looked away from the healer! I had seen a woman's arm grow out even to the other, had my eardrum healed when doctors said it wouldn't, and watched Him deliver over and over. so you will never convince me of any other idea! I just want you to know in a time like this on a day like today, he can Cleanse you inside and out, and he is waiting for the opportunity! Man has failed, again! Mans inability is God's Opportunity! I love you!

https://youtu.be/fWxCL4ROıcc[1]

---

1. Bishops, Clean Inside

Day 213

I will not operate in fear! Fear has no place in my mind or spirit, and it will not control my walk! This must be your position for your faith to shine through! God hasn't given it to you, so stop trying to claim it! Walk in love, joy, and peace today! It doesn't matter how the attack comes if you're prepared for it! Now fight and win! There is much to be done still! I love you!

https://youtu.be/TKsNCQBPHWM[1]

---

1. Colorado Mass Choir -Topic, Stir Up '98

Day 214

God is still able! He already has told us we win! Now just believe! Expect your exceeding and abundantly above all you can ask or think! Walk into today with Victory expected! I love you!

https://youtu.be/7YWaZayvJIA[1]

---

1. Tyscot, "He's Able" - Voices of Unity featuring Darwin Hobbs

Day 215

You may be in the fire, but when you make it through, you will be pure gold! The fire isn't here to destroy you! It's here to separate you from the impurities and things that lessen your value. Be encouraged! You will be more precious than gold when you come through! Just hold on! I love you!

(Oldie but goody)

https://youtu.be/l_Wno8WAggk[1]

---

1. Gospel Nostalgia, "Have You Been Tried In The Fire" (1982) Florida Mass Choir

Day 216

Do you feel it? I told you he wouldn't leave you! If you don't, take a moment and sit quietly and ask Jesus to show you He is there! Make sure you have some time, though, and you can't blame me for the result! You can't blame Him for being late either. So do it now! You win today because He is moving with you! I love you!

https://youtu.be/srGIp4LO-XM[1]

---

1. Tori Kelly, Tori Kelly - Never Alone (Official Live Video)

Day 217

God is great and greatly to be praised! His Will will be done! It's time to get closer to Him and know him! It's only He who can deliver us, and His healing power is here! Praise Him through it! He is worthy! I love you!

https://youtu.be/QvqLdWtVjIQ[1]

---

1. Tyscot, Deitrick Haddon's LXW - Great God

Day 218

You will make it through! You will survive! Stand up and keep moving forward! He didn't bring you this far to leave you! Your rainbow is there! The promise is to be fulfilled in you! I love you!

https://youtu.be/w3yH9SUAvJQ[1]

---

1. Lefon Briggs, John P. Kee "SURVIVE"

Day 219

C ontinue to press towards the mark! We cannot stop now, no matter the situation! He is our hope, and we look to Him for our help! Jesus has allowed us to see this day. So now, let's press into it and win the day! I love you!

https://youtu.be/glvWYbCT-qg[1]

---

1. Aaronhamptongospelbroadcast, I'm Going On - The Commissioned Reunion "Live" CD Album

Day 220

Are you going through too much to worship God? Has your investment in worship built up a standard in you to go through? I have seen too much, experienced too much, and overcome too much to stop worshipping now! If your worship is real, time to let Jesus know his place in your life! It will change the atmosphere around you now! I love you!

https://youtu.be/ChupmceWgpk[1]

---

1. Robbieatnsudotcom, My Worship Is For Real by Bishop Larry D. Trotter and Sweet Holy Spirit Combined Choirs

Day 221

W ho won? You did when you decided to walk with Jesus into this day! Now let's win this week by winning this first hour! You serve a great God who doesn't give up leads and can make Incredible comebacks for you when you put him in the game! You will accomplish everything you set out to! Speak it and then live it! I love you!

https://youtu.be/QvqLdWtVjIQ[1]

---

1. Tyscot, Deitrick Haddon's LXW - Great God

Day 222

P ress on! You will get through! You will overcome! Don't stop now! I know it seems harder than you thought, but you're almost to your breakthrough! No matter how hard you think it is, for you, the promises of God are greater than your struggle! See your victory today! I love you!

https://youtu.be/NIBx8ZbLMuk[1]

---

1. Gospel Nostalgia, "Overcome" (1982) D. J. Rogers

Day 223

This morning we thank God for mercy. He is always covering us in forgiveness, not to feel the weight of the sin we have repented of. Have you ever imagined how much you deserve for your own bad decisions, but yet He takes me in and covers me! I love Him, and I give my worship to Him! I know many of you are going through trials, but I have taken the stance like Job and say, "though He slay me, yet will I trust Him!" I know I am going through, but He has so much more waiting for me that I will press through! So I stand here calling His name! Will you do the same? I love you!

https://youtu.be/n4SpgUHk5lw[1]

1. Blazian2006, Calling My Name- Timiney Figueroa

Day 224

Just win! No other thoughts or options! You've been set up for success, and you may not have seen it, but know this, God has already ordered your next move! He won! Let your praise today reflect your Faith's knowledge that you have overcome, and you have the Victory! I love you!

https://youtu.be/KjkqPDv_Xgg[1]

---

1. Cheek Life, Commissioned - Victory

Day 225

You may think that no one cares and that you don't matter. This message is proof that you're mistaken and that Jesus loves you and thinks about you. Why else would you be reading this now during that thought process? Even though we live to love others, he cares so much for you that his blood was the sacrifice to ensure that YOU were covered! It feels good when someone really loves you enough to focus on, concentrate on, and cater to you, so why do you think Jesus does it for you? Exactly! I love you too!

https://youtu.be/R_EWDoaQm9Y[1]

---

1. Cheek Life, Commissioned - Jesus Cares

Day 226

S how what you want! Give the love you want to receive today!
Someone needs you to! If you can make someone feel the love you
desire, you allow God to show up in you and give you payment in return!
I love you, so love someone else! Be blessed!

https://youtu.be/Ve3jnAsdYfk[1]

---

1. Alexjackswing, Company - Love's In Need Of Love (1993)

Day 227

I don't know about you, but it sometimes irritates me when I buy someone something, and they waste it or don't use it! Especially when you know they really needed it and they just let it go to waste. Well, if that's you too, let's not let our heavenly father feel the same way! He gave us what we needed before we even knew we needed it! He paid a high price for it, and now he watches as it gets wasted and unused! Yes, it is a happy resurrection Sunday but make sure it means more than good food and some eggs! Jesus is the light and life! He came to light our way through times like these, so make sure you use the gift given! I love you!

https://youtu.be/DnTyNZEVs2U[1]

1. Robbieatnsudotcom, The Light by Ricky Dillard and New G

Day 228

The memory of how you've treated someone will carry longer than the message you preach! Make sure your salvation is remembered in the love you give in as much as the lessons you teach! Life is too short to be still holding petty grudges and having middle school-like interactions! The love of Jesus is your priority! By the way, I love you!

https://youtu.be/e5sAf42hdWA[1]

---

1. Liltg7, Canton Jones - Stay Saved + LYRICS (Music Video)

Day 229

S hort message today, Jesus is in the boat with you! The storm your facing becomes another testimony today because His peace will see you through! I love you!

https://youtu.be/_3VYlv207Wc[1]

---

1. Gospel Tunes, Yolanda Adams - Through The Storm

Day 230

G et up! Get focused! Don't stop! Back on your grind! Did you think because the opponent changed, the fight would too? Not so! Another victim is standing in front of you! No virus, disease, or problem can defeat a Jesus who is pleading for you to let him loose on your cares! It's time to win! Let's go!

https://youtu.be/JkRO8Vswcoo[1]

---

1. Bigsing74, WE MADE IT HEZEKIAH WALKER

Day 231

You will survive! Say that to yourself and believe it! I will survive! Your win must start with your own mind! No doubt, only faith, and belief! No buts! And so you know, heaven is the ultimate victory, but I have some work to finish here first so, I Will Survive! I love you!

https://youtu.be/w3yH9SUAvJQ[1]

---

1. Lefon Briggs, John P. Kee "SURVIVE"

Day 232

I can't know the owner of all food and supplies and still be worried! He said, take only what you need, for I provide manna for you daily. He will provide! Even though the enemy has attacked fiercely, all things work together for the good of them that love the Lord! Who will praise Him through even a pandemic!? I will shout into my next victory! How about you? I love you!

https://youtu.be/LEarvcRRHeI[1]

---

1. Tabernacle Christian Center RTP, For My Good, Judah Band Lyrics

Day 233

I t's not about you! It never was! When you begin to live this and try to be a blessing more than getting a blessing, you will find that the Lord pours more into you! You will be more fruitful, and the seeds you plant will yield good fruit. Give love, kindness, affection, and help freely. Even when you feel you're the one who needs it, I promise that Jesus will water you, and your life will be blessed! I love you!

https://youtu.be/B40bL4TFQ28[1]

---

1. Love Nest, Sow A Seed Of Love : Charles Woolfork & The Praise Covenant Choir

Day 234

You may feel that you don't have enough left today, but I am reminding you that Jesus is your I Am! He is the extra you need! He is your finisher, deliverer, strength, peace, joy, explanation, reason, your present help, antibiotic to the sickness of this world, your power, and so much more! You can because He is! Now go win! Hard to lose when your ringer is Jesus! I love you!

https://youtu.be/JAX7TXvQZoU[1]

---

1. Kerry Robinson, "I AM" by Eddie James

Day 235

I thank God I'm saved! I remember what he brought me out of and what I avoided because of his grace! I know how much he rescued me from, and I am thankful for his grace and mercy! Enough about me! How about you! Celebrate your salvation this morning! I love you!

https://youtu.be/C64oYCnYvqU[1]

---

1. Gospel Tunes, 'We Remember (Medley)' Thomas Whitfield featuring The Whitfield Company

Day 236

You have been built for this! Don't let the attack on your mind cause you to forget that if you allow the strength in you, the Holy Ghost, to work, you will come out of this fire without even a smell of smoke! There is nothing too harsh for God! He can even make your toilet paper last! Lol. No panic, just praise! You have been through bad before so stand on your testimonies! I love you!

https://youtu.be/5Tbk_a7HKiA[1]

---

1. Myron Williams, Bishop Richard "Mr. Clean" White (I'm Glad I Don't Look Like What I Been Through)

Day 237

Now is not the time for you to give up! You've heard so many things. You don't know what to believe, you're feeling discouraged, and isolation isn't making it any easier. It's time to realize that God provided for his people miraculously whenever the world was under judgment throughout history! We agree and proclaim your emancipation from the despair and fear now! Just Hold on and stay in his will! You will overcome! I love you!

https://youtu.be/2Y6Z-3jq4X8[1]

---

1. Men of Standard - Topic, In Your Will

Day 238

I have plans that I am working for, but I am living this life ultimately to see Jesus! It is important to me that I'm saved and that my life shows the love of Christ because I refuse to let anything keep me from my goal! If your goal is the same, let someone know today what your plans are! Live it more than saying it, though! Get right church, and let's go home when it's time! I love you!

https://youtu.be/TXqRBQqEFUo[1]

---

1. Robbieatnsudotcom, He'll Welcome Me by The New Life Community Choir featuring Pastor John P. Kee

Day 239

Revive means to make alive again or to "quicken," which means to jolt with power to cause to move or work. When we ask for revival, we need to expect to be doing more than before after it has come! If you have been expecting revival, then God is expecting results after! Time to walk into what we asked for! Let's move! Revival can begin today, but what is dead must wake up and live again! Purpose, gifts, dreams, work! Wake up now and be quickened! I love you!

https://youtu.be/Rl3sjZ3WdoY[1]

---

1. Gospelmusicchannel8, Dorinda Clark-Cole-Back To You

Day 240

Now isn't the time to stand still! Get up and let's go get it! Winning is in your DNA because the Blood of Jesus now runs the course all through you! Your destiny is to win, so go conquer! It's your time! I love you!

https://youtu.be/ADGnIi9KrLQ[1]

---

1. Mary Mary TV, Mary Mary - Go Get It (Official Video)

Day 241

I feel a little churchy this morning! What do I mean? I messed up and took a second to think about the goodness of Jesus! Remember this, It Was Never About You! You've been brought out for a purpose greater than you, so it's time to worship, praise, and testify to his goodness so the world can see his glory! Time out from waiting for someone else to get you excited! Let what God did for you be enough this morning! I started this message at 530am and had to come back to it now! If you understand why then you should be moving now! I love you!

https://youtu.be/K9Qb3lgoEKE[1]

---

1. Account5able, Tye Tribbett Praise Break YouTube

Day 242

Now let's let the saviour give you a pep in your step today! He is moving in you right now! He is shining in you, even if you feel like your battling! He is showing up through everything in you! So let him shine! Love you!

https://youtu.be/DnTyNZEVs2U[1]

---

1. Robbieatnsudotcom, The Light by Ricky Dillard and New G

Day 243

A woman named Louisa Stead wrote the song, "Tis So Sweet to Trust in Jesus... Oh, for Grace to Trust Him More." It was written when she had just lost her husband, who left her and her little girl alone. This impacted her ability to continue to do missionary work and just live due to her health issues. Even though she looked into the face of uncertainty, she wrote a song saying, "I am going to trust you more now, Lord!" How powerful it is to fall into more trust than anger and doubt when life's hard times hit you! Jesus wants that place in your life because his grace is sufficient for thee! Trust him today! I love you!

https://youtu.be/-7f-_HOjkWI[1]

1. Cheek Life, Commissioned - 'Tis So Sweet

Day 244

Now's the time to love! There are a lot of scared and hurting people. Although you can't hug, hold, or physically be there for many, we must find ways to love our neighbors. It's popular to be selfish and worry about your own in our world now, and the God in you must shine through. What will you do to show God's love today? I love you!

https://youtu.be/Ve3jnAsdYfk[1]

---

1. Alexjackswing, Company - Love's In Need Of Love (1993)

Day 245

We serve a mender of broken hearts! Jesus has already begun to put you back together again! Where you are weak, He is strong, and He completes your puzzle! Feel His moving in your broken places! Just start with the name that has the power to change everything, Jesus! I promise it starts your healing process now! I love you!

https://youtu.be/pSUu3H3rFQQ[1]

---

1. Indiana Bible College, Broken/Don't Pass Me By | He Knows

Day 246

Winning today is your choice now! You decide! Will you let God's plan come first and kick down life's doors and claim your day, or will you walk into the day, letting it toss you around? I will have a brighter day than yesterday! Even if yesterday was great, today will be better! We win because Jesus won! I love you!

https://youtu.be/OASpgmC-TsY[1]

---

1. Kirk Franklin, Brighter Day

Day 247

Hold on! Don't let go! Keep pressing! Don't believe your eyes and ears! Rely on your faith and what your spirit is leading you to! Time out for the enemy convincing you that you've failed or that this is another door closed! All things work together for the good of them that love the Lord. Your change begins today! Love will prevail! God said he is love, and if you know him and have him, you have love, which means the Love or the God you have will win for you! Today Mark's your Victory day! I love you!

https://youtu.be/InR9jHmVvIM[1]

---

1. Kaiabrown, For The Good of Them - Rev Milton Brunson

Day 248

His love will overwhelm you if you allow Him to love you! Today, concentrate on realizing that you didn't have to earn it, and He loves you more every day! Feel His arms wrapped around you even before you face any trial this day! He loves you and I do too!

https://youtu.be/1LngPIjfsiM[1]

---

1. Willie Ellebie Gospel Channel, Breath Away - Kirk Franklin presents One Nation Crew

Day 249

S top waiting for your situation to decide your fate! Tell it you've got the Victory! Dance your results into reality! Time to take control! In Jesus, you live, move, and have your existence, which means the ultimate winner consumes you! You already won! That step you just took means your closer to your win! Praise Him! I love you!

https://youtu.be/g84ONP8Xdng[1]

---

1. William LaVant, Lillian Lloyd - I've Got The Victory (Praise Break)

Day 250

It has never been about what you have to offer but rather your willingness! Our hang-ups about being good enough or bringing enough to the table are distractions to the purpose God has designed you for. Yes, you have to practice, read, work and put forth the effort, but your beginning comes from a God who has already designed you for it! The next time you worry about should it be you, ask yourself why was it Him! Jesus exchanged everything you need for the filthy rags you possessed! I love you!

https://youtu.be/28xqdcHmJ94[1]

---

1. Favorite Artists, Bebe & Cece Winans - Best of Bebe & Cece Winans - In Return

Day 251

J esus is everything to me! I realize more of Him is what I need in every situation, so I search for more of Him! As you face today, reach for more of Him!

https://youtu.be/Tk8dMEn3PJY[1]

---

1. Denzeldavon2, Tye Tribbett & G.A. | Everything Part I,Part II / Bow Before The King

Day 252

If you need strength this morning, take a moment to meditate on all of the good things God has done for you. When the stirring inside you moves you to tears of joy, realize the Joy that the Holy Ghost just deposited in you is your strength! The joy of the Lord is my strength; walk in it! It will help you win the day! I love you!

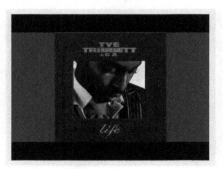

https://youtu.be/Uml_H_3Xbag[1]

---

1. Tye Tribbett, My Joy

Day 253

You are remembered! God is right there! He will not leave you! If you hadn't heard from Him when was the last time you read His word? That's how you dial His number! Prayer is then the conversation after. Hide His word in your heart, and you will realize He is always there! I love you!

https://youtu.be/Xh-hg7hCzuo[1]

---

1. Tonex - Topic, God Has Not 4got

Day 254

You are exactly where God wants and needs you to be! Stop doubting that your ready or that you heard right, or that you are in the right place! He has prepared you for such a time as this! He intends that you walk into your purpose at this perfect timing! Hey, destiny looks good on you! Now go get it! I love you!

https://youtu.be/VH3foellNv8[1]

---

1. Travis Greene, Travis Greene - Intentional (Official Music Video)

Day 255

In a war, you need soldiers to fight with you to win! Are you a willing soldier in this battle we face? Are you associated with true soldiers helping you win this battle? Important questions because God gave you armour and a sword, and believe me, the time for its use is now! New decade, fierce confrontations coming! It's time to win! This is a war cry! I love you!

https://youtu.be/7b9kzfP3NPQ[1]

---

1. Phillip Lewis, WAR CRY - Micah Stampley - Where My Warriors At - Calling All The Warriors!

Day 256

W here is your faith? Time to activate it! A mustard seed is small, but it is one of the fastest-growing spices and grows over 6ft tall in a few months. You may have seed faith to begin, but when Jesus is involved, it will explode into great faith if you activate Him with it! So what you have believed for this morning, let's agree! Time to move that mountain! I love you!

https://youtu.be/ogwYqlWc86Y[1]

---

1. Li'CalHon, Something to Sing About Move That Mountain

Day 257

Don't lose your grip! Hold on! God has you! There is nothing you can't make it through! Those who feel you're at the end of your rope and slipping realize it was never the rope that was holding you in the first place! Safe in His arms! I love you!

https://youtu.be/3IZAVUino1U[1]

---

1. Geivevo, GEI - Hang On ft. Kierra Sheard (Official Video)

Day 258

You're still not alone! The enemy wants your mind to believe you can cause God not to want you, but I'm here to tell you God is faithful and is whispering to you, "Just look up!" His hand is still extended, waiting for you to grab so he can pull you through! Get your mind right! Fight your own emotions and let Jesus soothe your mind! Hear me! He cares for you! I love you!

https://youtu.be/oaUJSpqyBpI[1]

---

1. JesusFreak18102, Nobody Cared with lyrics!-Canton Jones(PLEASE COMMENT!)

Day 259

He is worthy and a great deliverer! I refuse to live without Him! I couldn't if I wanted to because I am drawn to Him! How about you? Your reading this message, so He already gave you the first blessing! Will you praise him and take him with you all day or leave him at home? There is no way I could live without Him! I love you!

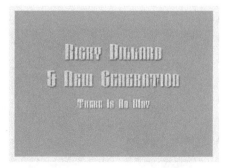

https://youtu.be/JUrje9Bw5mM[1]

---

1. PeculiarPrayze, Ricky Dillard & New Generation - There Is No Way

Day 260

Tell your storm it's time for it to leave! Speak to it in power and know it has to listen! Yes, the attack has been real, but Greater is He that is in you than he that is behind the weapons that can't work against you! The enemy sought to ruin you, your name, and your vision, but he forgot that all things work together for the good of them that love God! Put your umbrellas away, and let's see the SON work! I love you!

https://youtu.be/Rfoz6ihWUfI[1]

---

1. TheReelsofJoy, I Told The Storm - Greg O'Quin

Day 261

No worries this morning! Put them out of your mind! It's working in your favor already! Jesus is moving on your behalf right now! Why? Because you asked, and He heard you! Let your spirit feel his movement, and let's agree and praise Him for it! It's working out for you! I love you!

https://youtu.be/ZzbKwcC-Xmo[1]

---

1. Vashawnmitchell, VaShawn Mitchell - Turning Around for Me (Live)

Day 262

Walk in your joy for today! The joy of the Lord is your strength! I know you need more of that! Allow the Holy Ghost to give you joy! How? Release your worries and cares to him now! You've tried it your way, and it's left you stressed and miserable! Now tell Him, "these are yours, and I will take your joy today," and feel your day change! I love you!

https://youtu.be/u-Xx6UEUYJs[1]

Day 263

Why not today, and why not now? God has given you a new morning and a new start. So why isn't it your turn? Take it! Thank Him for it now, and get your victory! The world is not going to give it to you! Jesus has restored you, so you have everything you need to win! Right now! Today! I love you!

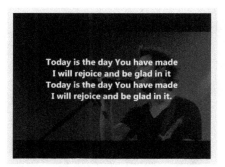

https://youtu.be/XH09MwYcgfg[1]

---

1. TheAlexloklok, Today Is The Day (Lincoln Brewster) - LYRICS

Day 264

There is no doubt that our healer is pulling us through! He did not bring us this far to leave us now! Fight your thoughts of isolation and loneliness! Being by yourself doesn't mean you're alone! ?? Did you get the wisdom of that? He is with you until the end! Right there, holding on to you to pull you through! I love you!

https://youtu.be/J9xQhNoRpFw[1]

---

1. Jermaine Dolly - Topic, Pull Us Through

Day 265

Your loved unconditionally! You can win today because no matter what you face, you have a saviour who can love you through it! His love strengthens and carries! When your heart feels like it's in pieces, the love of Jesus can put those pieces back together! You didn't earn it! He loved you enough to give it in spite of you! Go win, knowing there is love backing you up! I love you!

https://youtu.be/RBzxTYW5LGU[1]

---

1. Kadeem Graves, Unconditional - Fred Hammond & Radical For Christ

Day 266

My worship helped me through a tough day yesterday. I thank God for the relationship I have with Him! Jesus is! That's the personal translation of Him being the I am! Make it personal this morning a d worship him! I will worship Him because he is the completion of my needs and the finish of my story! Let's go in! I love you!

https://youtu.be/Ef4pDWL8wsM[1]

---

1. Emanuel Roro, Kanye West Sunday Service - "hallelujah, salvation, and glory" (Live From LA)

Day 267

Who's gonna do it? Jesus will! All faith and no doubt! It's that simple if you obey Him and just believe! That is all! I love you!

https://youtu.be/-6RVdlXquuw[1]

---

1. Anita Wilson, Anita Wilson - Jesus Will (LIVE)

Day 268

Your free! Jesus doesn't half do anything, which means when He freed you, when He opened your door, when He healed you, when He delivered you, you were completely let go, completely promoted, completely healed, completely moved to higher ground! I will not argue semantics or what your eyes are experiencing right now! It's up to you to walk in it and praise Him equal to the Blessing! I love you!

https://youtu.be/qOx2YNuakFo[1]

---

1.   Entertainment One Nashville, Todd Dulaney - Free Worshipper (AUDIO ONLY)

Day 269

D o you have the great assurance that Jesus is on your side? If the answer is yes, then raise your hands if you're sure! Take this moment to acknowledge the savior! If not, we need to talk! You will not make it without him! He is my fire prevention plan! You need one too! I love you!

https://youtu.be/xd0e2VsPwXM[1]

---

1. Tony Lee - Topic, Raise Your Hands

Day 270

I woke up singing this song, "Lord I Lift Your Name on High"! Praise and worship were in my spirit, and I was worshiping in my dream, and it feels amazing to have praise on your lips when you get up for the day. This isn't to say how God I am for doing this but instead to say how good God is that my spirit continues to worship him even as I sleep! Let your spirit salute Him all day! Let your very subconscious sing his praises, and it will create a presence of joy that nothing can shake. Troubles may come, but that joy will be your strength! Lift Him up! I love you!

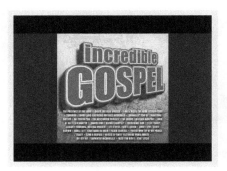

https://youtu.be/JtSlESK8kBk[1]

---

1. DonnieMcClurkinShow, Lord, I Lift Your Name On High

Day 271

If you need rest, restoration, deliverance, or peace, God is waiting to give it to you. Whatever you are doing right now, stop, take a second to hear God speak to you! Get what he is waiting to drop on you! He is able! I love you!

https://youtu.be/KSEBT8EDTuE[1]

---

1. Yana212, he's able darwin hobbs and detrick haddon

Day 272

You will win the day today, but first, you have to make the decision right now to let God work it out! Your involvement must be limited to His orders. You have other work to do, so leave the situation to God like you said you would when you prayed about it and let Him work it out! Jesus has already moved on your behalf; now let Him finish! You will win! I love you!

https://youtu.be/f58fsLTtnQk[1]

---

1. Gospel Tunes, "He'll Work It Out" Min. Charles Woolfork & Praise Covenant Choir

Day 273

Your 2020 can be better because no matter what, you ended 2019 in He still loves you! It's time to walk in his love! It surrounds you! I love you too!

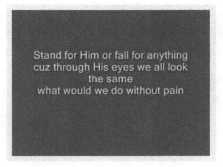

https://youtu.be/uIDZmXb-r7Q[1]

---

1. OzarkTiger076, Fighting Temptations He Still Loves Me Lyrics

Day 274

A true relationship has a root in love. If there is no love, it usually doesn't last or isn't rewarding and doesn't satisfy. What I'm saying this morning is this, "I'm in love with Jesus!" You don't have to know the whole story, but just know this, I'm not even sending this message without Him! My life has been enhanced and straightened by Him, and I owe Him my life! Take a moment to answer this, "Is your relationship built on love?" If so, tell Him you love Him! I love you too!

https://youtu.be/bA_DSJ8vAeQ[1]

---

1. Wgeorge84, I'm in Love with Jesus by New Direction

Day 275

I have chosen to lean on Jesus! So much so that if He moves, I will fall! I depend on his support, and I'm standing on his promises! You have a choice today! Lean on the one who created it all or keep depending on your flawed, limited mind and ability. The choice seems easy to me, but you have to make it! I love you!

https://youtu.be/vCCi8CnwDv4[1]

---

1. Kadeem Graves, If You Move, I'll Fall - The Bolton Brothers

Day 276

We live to live again! As much as God can bless us here, our reward remains to dwell with him forever! It hurts to lose loved ones here but to know they have received the reward we look forward to is comforting! May God's peace cover the hearts of those suffering loss this morning. Now let's gain our reward and see them again! Holiness is right, y'all! I love you!

https://youtu.be/mQO3UbZmwww[1]

---

1. Daryl Coley - Topic, To Live Is Christ

Day 277

When you are really in love, there is nearly nothing you wouldn't do to make the object of your affection happy. You would go out of your way to make sure they are completely taken care of, pleased, satisfied, cared for, safe, or recovered. We say we are in love with Jesus, and he is the object of our affection. Are we treating him like this? Ouch, or Amen! What's your response? I love you!

https://youtu.be/oCAY_qeDo-w[1]

---

1. Trial, Most Beautiful / So In Love (feat. Chandler Moore) - Maverick City Music | TRIBL Music

Day 278

Your heart is where Jesus wants to live. Is He welcomed there? He can only stay there if it's full of love, forgiveness, and faith. Have you furnished your heart with these? It's time to prepare your heart if it isn't already! It would be a shame to either have Him not welcomed or for him to be served an eviction notice. Check your heart! I love you!

https://youtu.be/FgspIyOiPo4[1]

---

1. Trial, My Heart Your Home (feat. Alton Eugene & Chandler Moore) - Maverick City | TRIBL

Day 279

Who told you to stop? Who said you were done? I didn't hear Jesus say, "The End!" Today is just one more canvas for God to paint your destiny's next masterpiece! Give praise, gird up, and win 11/4/19! I love you

https://youtu.be/aO9qJpX_BVc[1]

---

1. Mizzpinkc, It's Not Over (When God Is in It) feat. James Fortune & Jason Nelson

Day 280

We live to live again! As much as God can bless us here, our reward remains to dwell with him forever! It hurts to lose loved ones here but to know they have received the reward we look forward to is comforting! May God's peace cover the hearts of those suffering loss this morning. Now let's gain our reward and see them again! Holiness is right y'all! I love you!

https://youtu.be/mQO3UbZmwww[1]

---

1. Daryl Coley - Topic, To Live Is Christ

Day 281

My story has had some extraordinary circumstances and supernatural responses! God has been a miraculous healer, deliverer, counselor, friend, way maker, and defender. So I have no choice but to give him more than ordinary worship and praise! Why? Because I want to get closer, and I have learned to love because of him! How about you? Does your praise and worship match the expectations of your prayer response? If not, it should, and if so, give it to him now! I love you!

https://youtu.be/K_QiPd7d_A8[1]

---

1. Tyscot, Kelontae Gavin - No Ordinary Worship (Official Music Video)

Day 282

I made it out! I could have and should have been dead multiple times, but God's hands protected me, and I'm still here! Do you have that same testimony? Tell someone today, "It doesn't matter what I'm going through now because God has already shown me He can deliver!" Give Him the glory! I love you!

https://youtu.be/UzlRs4WCgIs[1]

---

1. Entertainment one Nashville, John P. Kee - I Made It Out (feat. Zacardi Cortez) (AUDIO)

Day 283

A question never asked doesn't get an answer is what they used to say. I thank God that he can read my tears, moans, movements, and my expressions! If you can't say a word, just wave your hands! He hears you, and He is moving on your behalf! He heard the question, so are you ready for the answer? Listen for it and move when it's time! Can he hear you? He already has! I love you!

Father just forgive us
Hear us when we
say

https://youtu.be/ZvSTrhYpeBs[1]

---

1. MsChan, Father Can You Hear Me - Lyrics

Day 284

Are you ready for God to give you overflow? We always ask for it but get upset when it doesn't happen, and God is saying, "You're not ready yet!" Just because it says you will not have room to receive doesn't mean you're not ready to receive! Did you get the wisdom of that? Be prepared to receive; humble heart, obedient to God's will, Holy living, giving heart, and a new made-up mind. Then you can receive the oil of God! I love you!

https://youtu.be/lYacUwQvpPE[1]

---

1. Joshua Rogers - Topic, Pour Your Oil

Day 285

You win! You overcome! Today is your testimonies good part! Believe it! Walk in the plan of Jesus because He never fails! Receive it and walk in it today! I love you!

https://youtu.be/4t7T5KTaHG8[1]

---

1. Gilbertmonk, Lowell Pye - Jesus Never Fails

Day 286

More of a challenge this morning than an inspiration: I pose this assignment to you, a whole day of being grateful! In word and action! Concentrate on not complaining or getting angry! Yes, it can start now because some of us have already failed the challenge, lol! God deserves a full day of our thanks! Even though Uncle Joe Joe ate the last piece of Sweet Potato pie, his third, and you didn't get any! Happy Thanksgiving, and I love you!

https://youtu.be/9-UdwIHSyqo[1]

---

1. Gospel Nostalgia, "Be Grateful" (Original)(1978) Walter Hawkins

Day 287

It may not feel easy, or it may feel like the weight of your situation has pressed on you more, but God said, "Be still! I'm working on it for you!" The weight you feel may be a shared one. Every circumstance isn't because of you, so the way God moves isn't always about you though it works for you. Your faith has to show up! I encourage you to hold on this morning! Pray for someone else today! Remember, it's not always about you! I love you!

https://youtu.be/ILK2vNeMwQI[1]

---

1. Travis Greene, Travis Greene - Be Still (Live Music Video)

Day 288

Through everything you may be facing this morning, I'm here to tell you Jesus still loves you! You are in His heart, and He wants what's best for you! Troubles don't ever mean his love is absent but clearly the opposite! It takes more to love someone at tough times and stress when they are hard to love, but He loves you anyway! Feel His love today and let it help you pull through! I love you too!

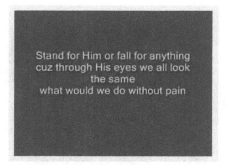

Stand for Him or fall for anything
cuz through His eyes we all look
the same
what would we do without pain

https://youtu.be/uIDZmXb-r7Q[1]

---

1. OzarkTiger076, Fighting Temptations He Still Loves Me Lyrics

Day 289

If you see this message, know that I am praying for you! It's never been about me but always about how to bless you! So this morning, take the time to cover someone in prayer. You don't have to know why or for what! The Holy Ghost will take care of that part. You're covered, so cover someone else. I love you!

https://youtu.be/QFIfoD9ZhLQ[1]

---

1. Alan Cooper, Cover Me-21:03 ft Fred Hammond, Smokie Norful, and J Moss

Day 290

I choose to worship! How about you? Why? You don't know my whole story! Because he is why the recent chapters look the way they do, he deserves all the praise! He is my all, and I love him! I dare you to take a memory inventory and, in your Holy Ghost imagination, think about if he wasn't in those moments! Your story would look so much different. I think you ought to praise him! I love you!

https://youtu.be/A1yK_L6hXiM[1]

---

1. The House of Hope, I Really Love The Lord song by Dr. E. Dewey Smith

Day 291

You begin this day with the memories of yesterday and the wonder of how to deal with today. It is easy to let your mind control your attitude. The directions you follow are mostly muscle memory. You are on automatic repeat, doing the same routine. Allow yourself a moment to concentrate and the greatness of God who is asking you to "Let me lead today." Think about how not even the greatest minds can comprehend how he has created everything to move in harmony and function in a world of chaos. He is so awesome, but yet he is focused on you now! Today isn't going to be routine! Your ordered steps will lead you into your desires and designed purpose! How incredible He is! I love you!

https://youtu.be/wdZViD4rxDE[1]

---

1. ABattles80, Kierra Sheard - Indescribable

Day 292

Weary from the battle? Wounded or shook from life's waves and winds? Right now, allow God to breathe into your life! Take a moment and speak life into yourself and believe the Holy Ghost is blowing in across your tiredness, your wounds, and your body now. Feel his recovery method moving in you as you prepare for the day! Relief is now in Jesus' name! I love you!

https://youtu.be/OXiKi-84RHs[1]

---

1. Cheek Life, Breathe into Me Oh Lord - Fred Hammond

Day 293

T his message is for you! If you have been through things that have made you bitter or angry and you can't live forward because your past is pulling backward. Your word this morning is this, "Your awake because of one reason. Your better starts now!" Audibly declare now that God has promised you Joy, and it's morning time! I love you, may God bless and keep you, make His face shine upon you, and be gracious unto you. May His countenance warm you this morning, and may His peace swallow you in the midst of your temporary storm!

https://youtu.be/lwO2qU6VK64[1]

---

1. Global Gospel Group, Jessica Reedy - Better

Day 294

We serve a miracle-working God! He has done so much, and I am thankful! Now we hold to his promises and look to what's to come! He is able to do whatever you need! Where is your faith! I love you!

https://youtu.be/S-DaM6033O8[1]

---

1. JJ Hairston, JJ Hairston - Official Video Miracle Worker (LIVE)

Day 295

Where ever you find yourself this morning, Jesus is there! He is pulling you out, opening the door, unlocking the chain, releasing you right now! You don't have to stay there! Get up and move out of harm's way! Your rescuer has shown up on time! Now rejoice and begin free today! I love you!

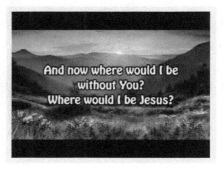

https://youtu.be/ybCOOCaHp5c[1]

---

1. dan4Jesus2012, Zach Williams - Rescue Story Lyrics

Day 296

It's time for the favor of God to make a difference in your life! Time for you to let go of the burden your eyesight brings and hold fast to the vision your faith has declared! It doesn't have to be comfortable, liked by others, or fair! All it has to be is yours! God promotes, blesses, and maintains us if we let him! I love you!

https://youtu.be/B4-fVK3cHvo[1]

---

1. Enemy of Knowing, Hezekiah Walker God Favored Me Ft Marvin Sapp And DJ Rodgers with lyricsHQ YouTube

Day 297

In a place of worship this morning. I love to think about his goodness because it always lets me see how worrying isn't necessary when going through trials and tough times! Concentrate on his goodness and allow the joy of the Lord to prepare for today! I love you!

https://youtu.be/IFi3tO1ezY4[1]

---

1. ICEdalightsout, Commissioned - I Love Thinking of U

Day 298

It's Hallelujah, anyhow! The battle doesn't get to change my Hallelujah! My situation doesn't get to change my Hallelujah! My haters can't take away my Hallelujah! Goe has earned my Hallelujah, and I will proclaim it through everything! My praise will carry through my positioning! So it's Hallelujah anyhow! I love you!

https://youtu.be/Cz-cpIR7fzY[1]

---

1. GospelMusicTV, Tamela Mann - Hallelujah

Day 299

He hasn't forgotten about you! No matter where you have opened your eyes, He is there! Let this remind you to climb to new heights and conquer new days because, with Jesus there, you can't lose! I love you!

https://youtu.be/3tTlFfQ3Qi8[1]

---

1. Antionette Harris - Topic, He Knows, He Cares

Day 300

You are ready! You will win today! There is no other finish! God ordained you to be right where you are so that your Victory today would jumpstart your future! It's time for you to walk in Victory! The word said it, "you can do all things through Christ..." now let him strengthen you! Win! I love you!

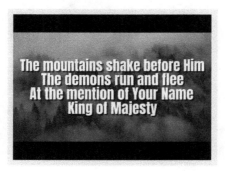

https://youtu.be/YVk55lbn8AQ[1]

---

1. ForGodSoLoved777, Great I Am | New Life Worship

Day 301

I t's time to give God praise! Where I could have been from the attacks on my life isn't where I woke up this morning, so I will Give Praise! Is that your testimony also? If it is, Let's thank our Saviour for his grace and mercy that's new this morning! I love you!

https://youtu.be/YXhDb_t_oVA[1]

---

1. Nogr8erluvthanhis, Marvin Sapp- Give Praise (Reprise)

Day 302

I am a witness that God can work out anything! If you don't know, you haven't tried him! I double-dog dare you to let go and let God take care of it. You will not be disappointed! Luke 1:37! Look for yourself! I love you!

https://youtu.be/Y3UPWUHi-Lo[1]

---

1. Praise Him Lyrics, Won't He Do It (Lyrics) Koryn Hawthorne ft. Roshon Fegan

Day 303

Your mind does a better job of condemning than anyone else can! It holds you hostage to your past and prevents your future from being right now! So we declare complete, spiritual control over our minds this morning! We run back to the one who gives us control and the ability to speak those things as they will now be, Jesus! I thought needing a long drawn out prayer, all my feelings and emotions into one word, Jesus! Call him now! Win now! Take control back! I love you!

https://youtu.be/Q6eCPNoxkHQ[1]

---

1. CDM Radio, Jesus - Le'Andria Johnson

Day 304

Have you wondered what it was like to be loved like you love others? Have you felt like you needed more love? Do you desire that feeling of love that envelops you and surrounds you when you know you don't deserve it? Well, Jesus has been trying to tell you just to let me love you like that, and then your life just feels different! Oh, by the way, I love you too!

https://youtu.be/ry3OR3F9huU[1]

---

1. CDM Radio, Kirk Franklin and the Family - Real Love

Day 305

The closer you get to Jesus, the more you feel his completeness! He fills your void and becomes your increase where you're lacking! I desire to get as close as possible! The best example I can say on getting closer is a puzzle when the last few pieces are found! I love you!

https://youtu.be/pgE7aI4utnQ[1]

---

1. Fred Hammond, Just To Be Close To You

Day 306

We are supposed to set our minds and thinking on God and Holy things so that the ways of this world cannot discourage or distract us. What are you thinking about this morning? Are you stressed about your job, family, health, or Bill's? Yes, you face some tough questions, but have you forgotten who woke you up to face them? When you've done all you can to stand, Stand! Take this opportunity to train your mind to think on Jesus! His peace will blow the enemy's stress away! I promise! I love you!

https://youtu.be/IFi3tO1ezY4[1]

---

1. Icedalightsout, Commissioned -I Love Thinking of U

Day 307

I don't believe He brought me this far to leave me! Therefore I must continue to press on! You may be standing at a wall that seems to be impassable or in a position that has you confused about how you got there. I promise you that you are in the perfect place for God to prove himself to you! Don't stop believing, and don't quit fighting! It's time to push through! I love you!

https://youtu.be/l5sbTKf7_NE[1]

---

1. Lowell Tye - Topic, Keep Pressing

Day 308

In all things, give thanks! Now that the holiday has passed will you celebrate him still? No matter what's going on around you right now, spend a moment of worship with him now! He desires a moment with you before you face this day! I promise you that it's necessary! I love you!

https://youtu.be/Wyvofsf3Qis[1]

---

1. Praise in the House Media, Worship Experience- William Murphy III

Day 309

Do you believe? Well, I do! I watched the power of God heal pancreatic cancer yesterday! Who wouldn't serve a God like that?! We aren't praising just because he healed but because his grace is deserving of it! When you believe He is enough and all you need, he does more to keep you in awe! I love you!

https://youtu.be/RqrsMVzjciI[1]

---

1. Maranda Curtis, Maranda Curtis - Nobody Like You Lord (Official Live)

Day 310

J ust a moment of reflection today! I will worship and praise all day because Jesus is everything to me! Nothing else matters because he is my I Am! He fills the blank! The fulfiller of my needs and desires! I will worship Him! I love you!

https://youtu.be/Tk8dMEn3PJY[1]

---

1. Denzeldavon2, Tye Tribbett & G.A. | Everything Part I,Part II / Bow Before The King

Day 311

As you begin this day, allow God to do what he promised. If you seek him first this day, he will set your feet on higher ground! You will rise above the problems, pain, and pettiness of the day, and God's grace will cover you everywhere you go! Make sure you seek him! Love you!

https://youtu.be/lg3VFxoooio[1]

---

1. TheBLSsingers, The Mississippi Mass Choir" I'm Pressing On!" (Plant My Feet On Higher Ground)!"

Day 312

It's already done! Your provider has said it, now walk in it! God, the author and finisher, has already told you it's finished. Now let your faith carry! I love you!

https://youtu.be/v2ImglEa93I[1]

---

1. Alaska Mass Choir feat. Dorinda Clark-Cole - Topic, Jehovah Jireh

Day 313

Declare this; I will trust him! Beyond my eyes! Beyond my fears! Beyond my failures! Beyond even my victories! I am standing in a place where my eyes want to be stable, but I know my faith will secure my pathway into my purpose and destiny! Jesus is my beacon, and I will not stop here! Time to move! I love you!

https://youtu.be/va5I6MOF-8M[1]

---

1. Mack Simpson Music Ministry, Anthony Brown & group therAPy - Trust In You (LYRICS)

Day 314

You must believe that it's alright before the storm hits! That way, your breakthrough is inevitable in your mind instead of being stressed and anxious waiting on it. How? Seek God daily, knowing he is a rewarder of them that diligently seek him. Read his word, worship him, fast, and pray. When your test comes, your seeking God will be a habit, and God's response will be normal! I love you!

https://youtu.be/GHw5uxPlRFo[1]

---

1. Godslittlegurl7, Hezekiah Walker Ft. John P. Kee ~ I'll Make It

Day 315

God knows exactly what you need and is working it out! You may not understand why, but if you trust Him, he will show you it is in your best interest! Trust the process, and you will be blessed, I promise! I know it's hard sometimes, but God is faithful! I love you!

https://youtu.be/Fb2wNc1Owpc[1]

---

1. Travis Greene, Travis Greene - Intentional (Lyric)

Day 316

Let your mind Stay in His presence today and feel his reign as He rains on you! Let your mind stay on His goodness and feel the purpose and direction he pours into your spirit today! Take advantage of every opportunity today! It's time to move! Its tour set up for a step up! I love you!

https://youtu.be/iJncObqrJR8[1]

---

1. GospelMusicTV, Earnest Pugh - Rain On Us

Day 317

You win because the battle and cost for your victory has already been taken care of! Stop walking into the day looking for what may happen and start going out with the expectation you have believed! It's time to adjust the atmosphere around you! Greater is he that is in you! I love you!

https://youtu.be/UdIPRdQYBFo[1]

---

1. Wess Morgan, Wess Morgan - You Paid It All - Official YouTube V

Day 318

No matter what you're going through, God has a plan, and it's working out for you! Sometimes the process hurts because it doesn't match our understanding. If we concentrate on the ending, we will see our gain coming! He will work it out! Just hold on! I love you!

https://youtu.be/KYiAEWSeYwY[1]

---

1. Robert Tyree, Sandra Crouch - God Has A Plan

Day 319

To win this day, you must trust In Jesus! Stop getting in your own way! You have tried your way, that doesn't work! Put your trust in him! Until you've tried him, you can't understand how much He makes the difference! He will not fail you! I love you!

https://youtu.be/L5ax_tY9pY8[1]

---

1. Ray Callaway, TRIED HIM & I KNOW HIM HOLY WILL by The Clark sisters

Day 320

It's time for the rain! You have felt the dirt and grime around you! You have felt the pressing and weight on you. You have felt the heat and feeling of confinement. You were being planted! Now feel the rain and watch the growth begin! You weren't comfortable, but you were placed where perfect germination could happen. Now, as God rains on you and feeds you, your roots will take hold, and you will outgrow what has seemed to keep you in place! Your new promotion, new healing, new purpose starts today! I love you!

https://youtu.be/ysssIPyWW-Y[1]

1. Entertainment One Nashville, Let It Rain - Bishop Paul S. Morton & The FGBCF Mass Choir

Day 321

As we see the Bible unfold before our eyes, we realize that we are ever closer to the return of Christ. There are still things that must happen, but the pace of these events has sped up. It is not a time of panic or fear, but one of awareness and preparation and joy! Like the old song says, "When I see Jesus, Amen!" Now, as you face this day, answer this question, are you ready? It's time to be in your word and sharing the salvation of the Lord to all so we can be with him when he comes! Let's be ready! I love you!

https://youtu.be/U93vR8R3qFI[1]

---

1. Cheek Life, Commissioned - Will You Be Ready?

Day 322

When they wonder how you got here or why you have what you have, all you have to tell them is, 'You don't know what this place took out of me!' Today is testimony day! Take 30 seconds right now to really take a memory inventory and reflect on how good Jesus has been to you! Ok, 60 seconds because 30 isn't long enough! I can't praise him enough, and I know it may be hard right now, but on the other side of going through, I will have another praise! I love you!

https://youtu.be/RagW-RcY_Go[1]

---

1. Jason Coward, Zacardi Cortez- You Don't know

Day 323

J esus wants you to win today! That happens by you following the plan designed to end in your victory. Now, listen to his directions, apply them to your plans for the day, win the day! All you have to do is take time to listen first! I know it's Christmas eve, and you have so much to do, but you have to take time to listen! I love you!

https://youtu.be/6qK5b_kokJE[1]

---

1. O'Neil Beckford, Speak to My Heart - Donnie McClurkin

Day 324

Have your eyes won? Do you falter because of how it looks going into today? Well, stop looking at it then! His blood has covered you, and His grace and mercy have justified you. The word says, "The just shall live by their faith!" It's time that all of those Sunday School lessons and Bible study lessons pay off! It's in you to stand, so Stand Therefore! Your faith will take you where your eyes would leave you to fail! Have faith in God! You win! I love you!

https://youtu.be/8RbSD9czoLc[1]

---

1. Kadeem Graves, The Just Shall Live - Walter Hawkins & The Love Center Choir

Day 325

No matter what you think you should have, have you been appreciative of what's already been given? Today we begin by being grateful for all God has done already! Most of us feel It's hard to give unappreciative people more, so why should we treat God the same? Thank Him this morning! I love you!

https://youtu.be/zPKFug6bNOI[1]

---

1. Nicky Savage, Le'Andria Johnson "Be Grateful" Hawkins Family Tribute

Day 326

Whatever it is, God will deliver on time! Hold on and believe your change is here! He will never leave you! It's time for Jesus to do what he does! I love you!

https://youtu.be/Scr3Yv8uCNw[1]

---

1. Demetrius26100, God Will Deliver The Williams Brothers

Day 327

I send messages because GOD has blessed me and whether good or bad times come, I have always felt him move in my life, so I promised to tell the world of His goodness. When you see or hear me worship, know there is a price paid for it. What is your story? Have you seen the glory of God in your life? Is your worship bought and paid for? If the answer is yes, then go ahead and give Him his due. If it is no, He is waiting for you to get out of your own way today and let Him drive. You will never be the same I promise! I love you!

https://youtu.be/ChupmceWgpk[1]

---

1. Robbieatnsudotcom, My Worship Is For Real by Bishop Larry D. Trotter and Sweet Holy Spirit Combined Choirs

Day 328

Today is your day! Say, "Overflow!" Your day of blessed beyond measure! Whether it is physical, spiritual, emotional, mental, or all of the above! I speak and declare God's healing, deliverance, promotion, and increase over you and everything you touch now! Why? Because Jesus said, I could! I love you!

https://youtu.be/jZjKIEJcbys[1]

---

1. Evdely WorshipLivingGod, BLESSINGS ON BLESSINGS ANTHONY BROWN & GROUP THERAPY By EydelyWorshipLivingGodChannel

Day 329

God heard you the first time! He has you covered! Let your praise help release your requests' arrival this morning! We fight with worship and praise today, and we believe God's blessings will land in overflow TODAY! I love you!

https://youtu.be/pnNP_fVjB9Y[1]

---

1. Mark T. Jackson, YOU COVERED ME - Dr. R.A. Vernon & "The Word" Church Praise Team, Timothy Reddick Lead

Day 330

It may have been a fight, but you got out! Give glory to God for your new beginning today! His mercy met your eyes opening! Praise him for new Victory! We win!

https://youtu.be/UzlRs4WCgIs[1]

---

1. Entertainment One Nashville, John P. Kee - I Made It Out (feat. Zacardi Cortez) (AUDIO)

Day 331

Don't step back now! You've come this far! Hold on! I promise you can make it! God's investment in you has matured, and it's time for you to cash in and reap the benefits! It's in you! Jesus wrote the chapter that said, you win! I love you!

https://youtu.be/9-h2chAdFWU[1]

---

1. Global Gospel Group, Bryan Popin - I Can Make It

Day 332

It's time to step into victory! It's time to win and not care who hates you for it! God said, you win, and the enemy can't stand it! Praise Jesus this morning! I'm glad the devil is mad! Do not stop till you get what you asked for! I love you!

https://youtu.be/6JLbsGgfpO4[1]

---

1. Tony Lee - Topic, The Devil Don't Like This

Day 333

Be free! Leave your burdens and cares at the feet of Jesus and walk in freedom today! Let him give you peace! It can be yours if you would only trust Him and step out of your own way! Grab it and keep it! It feels good to be free! I love you!

https://youtu.be/onoC8KAENSw[1]

---

1. Millennial Hardware, Freedom- Eddie James lyrics video

Day 334

Are you ready for change yet? We have seen many dark days because we have continued to attempt the same failing processes to change! Yes, anger has spilled over, and there will be consequences and adjustments after it all, but when the dust settles, what will be the change? We must return to a dependency on God's divine leadership and let His will lead us to make the necessary changes to unite broken people! Where there is no unity, there is no strength! Time out for trying to be the loudest voice in the room and turn to have United voices! It's the only way to make change! Of course, there will be those opposing it, but if we stand together with God in front, he will make them. I believe the Bible calls them "footstools!" But God first, unity, and then change! I love you!

https://youtu.be/OnyjgYcGJ2E[1]

---

1. WalterHawkins - Topic, Changed

Day 335

I t's time to seek God! In a time when the enemy is trying to attack, confuse, and tear apart everything we hold dear to us, Jesus is the answer! Lean on him, and you will make it, I promise! A proven help will prevail! I love you!

https://youtu.be/-bk5iRcphWY[1]

---

1. Josh Lopez, Josh Lopez & Mark Townsend- God you are God performed by Lisa Lopez and the CBC Choir

Day 336

You have an opportunity for another win because you have been blessed with a new day! Time to thank God and clear your plans with him. Then go win! Speak your Victory into the atmosphere and then walk in it! "I will be happy today!" "I will accomplish what I set out to do today! " "I will make a difference today! " Declare it and win! I love you!

https://youtu.be/oEws3aY3_zg[1]

---

1. Cheek Life, Commissioned - We Are Overcomers

Day 337

W alk into today's situation with the confidence that God is still able! He has done it before, which makes today another victory! It's already done! I love you!

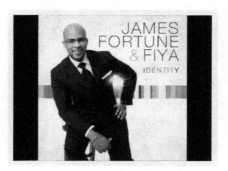

https://youtu.be/GFrVZCYVkrY[1]

---

1. Gospelmusicchannel8, James Fortune & Fiya-Still Able

Day 338

J esus never fails! You are accompanied by the greatest deliverer ever, and He said, "Step behind me and watch me work!" Now praise him and do what He said! I love you!

https://youtu.be/aflHUpeBcUo[1]

---

1. PeculiarPrayze, Kirk Franklin - (He Reigns) Our God Is An Awesome God

Day 339

You are standing in a place of possibilities! You know that man's inability is God's opportunity! The failure of what your eyes have seen will never equal the strength of Faith's ability! God has positioned you to win, so... GO WIN! Put him first, believe his plan, Go get it! Love you!

https://youtu.be/rDo2TFfmuvU[1]

---

1. John Smith, Nothing Is Impossible PlanetShakers ft Israel Houghton

Day 340

Now is not the time to keep to yourself! Your light must be seen! That is if you have a light! This world doesn't need better political representation and world view! It needs the redeemed to say so and live the love of Christ that draws people instead of the hypocrisy of a watered-down traditional-based lifestyle that can't stand in the storm! Time to let the power and glory of God be seen in our lives! Either say ouch or amen! Let's show what the word "Christian "is supposed to mean! Love you!

https://youtu.be/HP0IVATVB9Y[1]

---

1. Donnie Nelson, Isaac Carree ft. John P. Kee - We Are Not Ashamed

Day 341

You are not alone! You don't have to go anywhere else to find love! The enemy uses separation tactics like hunting lions to increase your anxiety and depression. But Jesus sent me to tell you He hasn't left you, and He cares for you! It may seem like no one loves or is concerned for you, but yes, my message changed today to speak to you! He loves you, and so do I! Have a day full of the love of Christ!

https://youtu.be/oaUJSpqyBpI[1]

---

1. JesusFreak18102, Nobody Cared with lyrics!-Canton Jones(PLEASE COMMENT!)

Day 342

It's Friday, so what's good about it? Have you measured the life shown by a Saviour who operated in mercy and grace? We didn't deserve it and proved unworthy daily. Yet Calvary stands as a reminder of the unmerited favour that God Grant's us! Your mercy renews every morning, and His blood has washed away our reasons for separation from Him! There is no greater love than His love for us! I heard you in my spirit! "Where is His love in a world that's suffering?" It's where it always has been, waiting for an unrepentant and unholy people to accept it to escape the recompense of sin that it has to be judged for! It is a Good Friday looking to a better Sunday! He loves you and I do too!

https://youtu.be/-aj2S_Fs_CY[1]

---

1. Pastor Hooks, No Greater Love - Fred Hammond (Free to Worship)

Day 343

Today, you win! No exceptions! Today is your Victory! We claim it now! God said it, I believe it, I'm walking in it! I love you!

https://youtu.be/OIun53iz6s4[1]

---

1. DonnieMcClurkinShow, Donnie McClurkin - We Are Victorious ft. Tye Tribbett (Official Video)

Day 344

G od loves you! No matter how bad yesterday went, His mercy renewed, and your eyes opened today! Now take advantage of that gift and destroy your adversary today! How? Love somebody else! That's the challenge! You're not unlovable to him, so make sure no one is unlovable to you! I LOVE YOU!

https://youtu.be/3aD8OKo7iIY[1]

---

1. Kirk Franklin, Kirk Franklin - Love Theory (Official Music Video)

Day 345

Through it all, I have learned I have a friend in Jesus! No pain, problem, situation, or person can keep him away! He thrives in my storms, and I wouldn't be able to send one message without his mercy being attached to it. I am in a place of worship, even though the test isn't over! Why? Because he slipped me the answers! He has them for you too! I love you!

https://youtu.be/7JXFg5KEoXg[1]

---

1. GospelMusicTV, Never Would've Made It - Marvin Sapp

Day 346

B e free! Whatever is trying to lock you up, hold you back, tie you down, be free now! You woke up this morning with the chain breaker on your side! Jesus is waiting for your permission to handle it now! Will you choose the insanity of your way again?! I pray, not! I love you!

https://youtu.be/-pD2zIuiC2g[1]

---

1. Tasha Cobbs Leonard, Tasha Cobbs - Break Every Chain (Lyrics)

Day 347

It's time to acknowledge who you serve! "For God, I live, and For God, I Die" used to be the anthem of a dedicated servant of God but in our current world, seeing this lifestyle is becoming harder and harder. So let the redeemed of the Lord say so! We serve an awesome God, and it's time to say so! I love you!

https://youtu.be/QvqLdWtVjIQ[1]

---

1. Tyscot, Deitrick Haddon's LXW - Great God

Day 348

They should have never counted you out! Your recovery and step up will be a story of legend! No one has to believe it but you! God has your Victory in His plan! Now win today! Walk in it today! Praise him for it today! Yesterday is gone, so all you need is today's view! I love you!

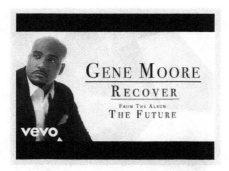

https://youtu.be/d4I_Y8r9DZo[1]

---

1. Gene Moore TV, Gene Moore - Recover (Audio)

Day 349

Your debt has been paid! Jesus made sure you were free of the penalty of your own doing and failure! So how will you repay him this morning? Give him a praise that's worthy of the value of your debt! Only you know how deep your debt was! That should cause someone to run today! I love you!

https://youtu.be/1lL8fGc8fMo[1]

_____

1. Kirk Franklin, Jesus Paid It All

Day 350

It's hard not to be cocky when you know who's fighting for you! Realize the odds are stacked in your favor! You may take a good blow but shake it off and stand tall! You've got the edge! The enemy thinks they've got you where they want you, but you've been set up for the win in reality! It's over, and you're victorious now! Love you!

https://youtu.be/OoDsTBACQWM[1]

---

1. Anthony Evans Entertainment, Fighting For Us Lyric Video - Anthony Evans

Day 351

I will win the day! Not because of how great I am but because of his amazing grace! The chains made for my imprisonment are now being used to climb out of where the enemy thought he had left me to die! The weapon was formed, but it was rendered useless as I walk in Victory! Can you see it? Look again! This time with your faith and eyes of expectancy! His blood has covered me, so I know I walk into today already a winner! You do the same! I love you!

https://youtu.be/Jbe7OruLk8I[1]

---

1. Alwaysforgiven821, Amazing Grace (My Chains are Gone) - Chris Tomlin (with lyrics)

Day 352

It's the day after Thanksgiving, but that should be an everyday occurrence. So let's give him an "I'm still here, and I'm glad" praise this morning! He is worthy! I love you!

https://youtu.be/lsMJtma8YIQ[1]

---

1. Entertainment One Nashville, Dorinda Clark Cole - Back To You (AUDIO ONLY) 2011 Light Records Single

Day 353

What are you waiting for? You've prayed, fasted, meditated, sought God, and been in your word, so you've positioned yourself correctly, but you're not moving! You know what and where you are supposed to be! Your hesitation is holding up your blessing! How many signs do you need? What if God waited for you to pray three times for something before starting to move on your behalf? Let's go! I love you!

https://youtu.be/3_gCeNWVVdY[1]

---

1. Eferem Hurdle, Edwin Hawkins Music & Arts Seminar Mass Choir - Call On Jesus

Day 354

He is saying this morning, "Keep moving because I am still in your steps!" He has not forsaken you! He will never leave you! Yea, though you walk through the valley of the shadow, You win because he won! I love you!

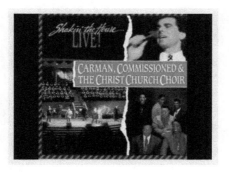

https://youtu.be/c8tSOi68Wv4[1]

---

1. Cheek Life, I Am Here - Commissioned 'Live'

Day 355

A new year doesn't matter if you carried the same old baggage into it! Renew your mind and walk in the grace He has gifted! You are as brand new as your mind is! Speak it, walk it, live it! It's your time! I love you, and Happy New Year!

https://youtu.be/lDUrIVGak-A[1]

---

1. PeculiarPrayze, Israel and New Breed - It's A New Season

Day 356

Point the way, Lord, and we will go! It's a new day and new week, which means today's Victory is important! We win by your design! Thank you in advance, Lord! Amen! I love you!

https://youtu.be/owYitgTT9vA[1]

---

1. Minjalewiser, Order My Steps (Salt Of The Earth).wmv

Day 357

What you felt you lost, God has set you up for the recovery! Let's win the day and begin to take back what the enemy TRIED to steal! He doesn't have the authority to take anything, and we declare now that we want it back! Start with a planning meeting with the Holy Ghost this morning, then add a moment of asking God's approval, then go get it! It is flip it Friday! The day we flipped the enemy's plans for us upside down! I love you!

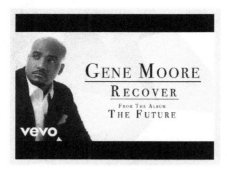

https://youtu.be/d4I_Y8r9DZo[1]

---

1. Gene Moore TV, Gene Moore - Recover (Audio)

Day 358

Today is just God's opportunity to be a right now God! Your situation is "In Process!" Praise him early! Watch God work today! No bad mood or attitude because my smile signifies my expectation! Love you!

https://youtu.be/FRyAyBwbTso[1]

---

1. Alaska Mass Choir feat. Dorinda Clark-Cole - Topic, [Reprise] Right Now God

Day 359

Your strength is here this morning! You asked for it, and Jesus is meeting you at your request right now! I'm encouraging you to hold on and feel Him filling your weak places! His love is great enough to grant your cries! Did you forget that your mercies renewed when you opened your eyes? Know Him is to know your added increase! I love you!

https://youtu.be/M7-XxVJNVHw[1]

---

1. Callow, Fred Hammond - A Song of Strength

Day 360

I f your happy and you know it, say Amen! What is there to be happy about? You're able to read this message. That means God's grace has blessed you to have one more day. Yesterday is defeated. You are set for progress and victory today. No matter what you're facing, the arms of Jesus are waiting for you to comfort and protect or celebrate with! You have a lot to be happy about! And even if you don't agree with me, praise Him anyway and watch what he does! I love you!

https://youtu.be/bTncJhkc8gA[1]

---

1. The Club Brand, C-Dub Remix- "Happy" (Tasha Cobbs/Pharrell Williams)

Day 361

Thank you, Jesus, for truly being the gift that keeps on giving! I will concentrate on being that example and practice my cheerful giving to be a blessing today! Why? Because He first gave me his all so I can be blessed! Merry Christmas, and I love you!

https://youtu.be/Y7CBq8QbpoA[1]

---

1. Rhino, CeeLo Green - Mary, Did You Know? (Official Audio)

Day 362

You made it! It doesn't matter what trials came and the problems you faced yesterday; God saw fit that you start new this morning! Take your new mercy and attack the day before it can attack you! Love you!

https://youtu.be/UzlRs4WCgIs [1]

---

1. Entertainment One Nashville, John P. Kee - I Made It Out (feat. Zacardi Cortez) (AUDIO)

Day 363

You may not have known what you were getting into when you asked God for that gift, that anointing, that ministry, or that testimony. Now after your inauguration, which is a transfer of power or control publicly, you wondered where all the haters, attacks, and problems came from. Take what you asked for, ante up and kick in like real men and women of God! It's time to go get it! Walk in it! I love you!

https://youtu.be/SqGjIKEhRxo[1]

---

1. Yolanda Adams - Topic, In the Midst of It All

Day 364

I want to remind you about a friend of mine this morning! He told me to tell you hi and that He Hope's to talk to you soon. He said you have the number so call Him! I'm pretty sure he already knows what you want to talk about! I have to go now! I am gonna finish talking to Jesus before I head out! Love you!

https://youtu.be/xlSZh-wsW6w[1]

---

1. Kirk Franklin, Something About The Name Jesus Pt. 2

Day 365

We are more than overcomers! We can't lose if we faint not! What does that mean? It doesn't mean you won't cry or you won't hurt or you won't suffer but it does mean those things are only temporary and part of a process which leads to victory here and in heaven! If you never have good days check your road! You may have missed the detour sign! I love you!

https://youtu.be/oEws3aY3_zg[1]

---

1. Cheek Life, Commissioned - We Are Overcomers

ABOUT THE AUTHOR

Pastor Adrean R. Young is a saved, sanctified, filled with the Holy Ghost and fire, servant of God. His life has been the greatest instrument in showing how God can use what you may think is ordinary to exhibit how extraordinary the power and love of God can be.

He is the oldest of three siblings, child of a career enlisted United States Air Force veteran, and one of the youngest in a very large family in northeast Ohio. It would have been easy for Adrean to disappear into the background. But, the calling on his life and a very loud personality refused to let that happen.

As a citizen of the world, a musician, athlete, history buff, and family-first guy, God's love was shown to him early and often through his parents, who would not give up on a stubborn kid who wanted it his way.

Presently a Pastor, husband, father, working man, counselor, friend, and now author, Pastor "A" is sharing the joy that God has given him.

facebook.com/min.adrean.young

twitter.com/quesosplace

instagram.com/quesosplace

CPSIA information can be obtained
at www.ICGtesting.com
Printed in the USA
LVHW080405240221
679709LV00010B/125